KHIVA

RIDE TO KHIVA

BY

ROBERT L. JEFFERSON, F.R.G.S.

AUTHOR OF "ROUGHING IT IN SIBERIA," ETC.

WITH FIFTY-ONE ILLUSTRATIONS

NEW YORK
NEW AMSTERDAM BOOK COMPANY
1900

b. (wit.)

ŚW|| HDRAWIE

TO

CHARLES PERCIVAL SISLEY, Esq.

WHOSE ACTIVE INTEREST AND ASSISTANCE

IN THE VARIOUS

TRANS-CONTINENTAL CYCLING JOURNEYS

I HAVE UNDERTAKEN

I DESIRE TO ACKNOWLEDGE

BY THIS DEDICATION

PREFACE

THE real reason why I rode a bicycle to Khiva was because so many people said it was impossible. That there was a certain amount of fascination in the idea I admit, for I have always been a keen admirer of the stalwart guardsman whose horseback ride across the desert of Kizilkum will be remembered long after his brave exploits in Egypt have been forgotten. My object was to emulate Captain Burnaby's ride to Khiva, but as a sportsman only. The future of Central Asia (such a problem in Burnaby's time) is now settled; but I am vain enough to think that, so far as Khiva itself is concerned, I shall be able in these pages to tell something which is new; namely, the present rapid decay and all too evident speedy demise of a once important Central Asian province. The Khanate of Khiva, which, twenty-five years ago, was so much talked about, is to-day of but small account—even to Russian administrators. Central Asian travellers have entirely ignored it for more than ten years, and in the Russian development schemes affecting Turkestan it takes no place. Under these circumstances, if I bring news of an almost forgotten part of the world which will be interesting to English readers, I shall not consider that my ride was undertaken uselessly.

ROBERT L. JEFFERSON

LONDON, *August*, 1899

CONTENTS

CHAPTER   PAGE

I. FROM CATFORD TRACK TO THE BELGIAN
FRONTIER 1

II. ON BELGIAN PAVÉ 10

III. ON THE BANKS OF THE RHINE . . 17

IV. ON THE BAVARIAN HILLS . . . 23

V. BY THE BLUE DANUBE . . . 32

VI. IN THE LAND OF THE UNGARN . . 44

VII. ACROSS THE CARPATHIANS . . . 53

VIII. AMONGST THE GALICIANS . . . 63

IX. ACROSS THE RUSSIAN FRONTIER . . 71

X. IN LITTLE RUSSIA 81

XI. A NIGHT WITH THE MOUJIKS . . 91

XII. ON THE CENTRAL RUSSIAN CHAUSSÉE . 101

XIII. TOWARDS EAST RUSSIA . . . 110

XIV. NIGNI-NOVGOROD THE FAMOUS . . 120

XV. BY THE SIDE OF THE VOLGA . . . 135

XVI. CAUGHT IN A DUST-STORM . . . 147

XVII. ON THE EDGE OF THE KHIRGHIZ STEPPES 157

XVIII. ON THE FRINGE OF THE DESERT . . 169

XIX. THE KARA KUM 178

CONTENTS

CHAPTER		PAGE
XX.	FORT NO. 1	186
XXI.	THE START ACROSS THE KIZIL KUM	195
XXII.	TROUBLE WITH THE BODYGUARD	203
XXIII.	A BRUSH WITH THE KHIRGHIZ	211
XXIV.	THE WELL OF BIA-MURAT	219
XXV.	PETRO-ALEXANDROVSK AT LAST	230
XXVI.	THE DESERT RIDE FINISHED	239
XXVII.	PETRO-ALEXANDROVSK	249
XXVIII.	THE GATES OF KHIVA	262
XXIX.	KHIVA THE DECAYING	273
XXX.	MY RECEPTION BY THE KHAN	285
XXXI.	HOMEWARD	302

LIST OF ILLUSTRATIONS

KHIVA	. . . . .	*Frontispiece*
THE START FROM CATFORD	. . .	*To face page* 4
EN ROUTE TO CALAIS	. . . .	,, ,, 4
COLOGNE	. . . . .	,, ,, 16
FRANKFORT-ON-MAIN	. . . .	,, ,, 16
AMONGST THE HUNGARIAN CYCLISTS	. .	,, ,, 40
A VINEYARD INSPECTOR IN OFFICIAL ROBES	.	,, ,, 52
IN THE CARPATHIANS	. . . .	,, ,, 58
A GALICIAN CONFIRMATION PROCESSION	. .	,, ,, 58
TYPES OF GALICIAN PEASANTS	. . .	,, ,, 68
DAMSELS OF LITTLE RUSSIA	. . .	,, ,, 80
A TYPICAL POLISH JEW	. . . .	,, ,, 80
THE MOUJIK AT SAMOVAR	. . .	,, ,, 94
THE DANCE, *A LA RUSSE*	. . .	,, ,, 94
A RELIGIOUS PROCESSION IN CENTRAL RUSSIA	.	,, ,, 112
SUNDAY IN CENTRAL RUSSIA	. . .	,, ,, 120
EAST RUSSIAN ARCHITECTURE	. . .	,, ,, 120
A FAMILY OF HAPPY TARTARS	. . .	,, ,, 138
OPEN PAPER OF THE RUSSIAN GEOGRAPHICAL SOCIETY	. . . . .	,, ,, 158
THE EUROPEAN-ASIATIC BORDER	. . .	,, ,, 170
THE BICYCLE CAUSES DEEP INTEREST	. .	,, ,, 170
KHIRGHIZ BEAUTIES OF THE MIDDLE HORDE	.	,, ,, 176
THE ROAD ACROSS THE KARA-KUM	. .	,, ,, 180
A KHIRGHIZ MEDICINE MAN	. . .	,, ,, 184
THE BANKS OF THE SYR-DARIA	. . .	,, ,, 190

THE FERRY AT FORT NO. I . . . *To face page* 190

A KHIRGHIZ WITCH . . . . ,, ,, 194

THE SHIP OF THE DESERT AS A CYCLIST ,, ,, 194

THE AUTHOR'S DRAGOMAN, OSMAN MURATR . ,, ,, 196

THROUGH THE SYR-DARIA SWAMP . . ,, ,, 196

THE HOSPITABLE KHIRGHIZ . . . ,, ,, 202

MUSIC IN THE KIBITKA . . . ,, ,, 202

IN THE DEEP SANDS . . . ,, ,, 210

A MIDDAY HALT . . . . ,, ,, 210

KIBITKA AT THE WELL OF BIA-MURAT . . ,, ,, 218

THE AUTHOR GETTING USED TO KHIRGHIZ LIFE ,, ,, 220

THE WELCOME WATER . . . . ,, ,, 220

STRANGE METHOD OF CURING KHIRGHIZ SICK ,, ,, 224

A SUMPTUOUS KIBITKA . . . . ,, ,, 228

THE LAST WELL ON THE DESERT . . . ,, ,, 228

THE LAST DESERT ENCAMPMENT . . . ,, ,, 236

THE WALLS OF KHIVA . . . . ,, ,, 236

THE GATE OF KHIVA, FROM WITHIN . . ,, ,, 254

A KHIVAN RECEPTION . . . . ,, ,, 254

THE PRIME MINISTER TO THE KHAN . . ,, ,, 272

A KHIVAN STREET . . . . ,, ,, 276

THE FAMOUS TOWER OF KHIVA . . . ,, ,, 276

THE GERMAN VILLAGE NEAR KHIVA . . ,, ,, 294

THE KHAN . . . . . ,, ,, 300

A NEW
RIDE TO KHIVA

CHAPTER I.

FROM CATFORD TRACK TO THE
BELGIAN FRONTIER

WHEN the cycle cavalcade, at least thirty
strong, debouched into the main road at
Rushey Green, Catford, a policeman standing at
the corner excited the wit of the wag of the party.

"Which way to Khiva?" asked the wag.

"First to the left, and straight on," replied the
guardian of the peace with promptitude, and he
was right in the main. First to the left it was
in order to make for the high road to Maidstone,
Ashford, and Dover, but there promised to be
many turnings before Khiva—nearly six thousand
miles away—would be reached.

B

The good people of Catford stared amusedly at the heavily laden bicycle which I rode. They wondered, perhaps, at the sight of so many wheelmen out so early in the morning, and the knot of labourers who had collected in front of the hostelry by Southend Pond cogitated, no doubt, as to the why and wherefore of so much hand-shaking and wishes for good luck on the part of many of those wheelmen who could go no further.

The month was April, and no one could desire a better cycling day than the one on which I commenced a ride which was to be fraught with so many difficulties and obstacles—difficulties and obstacles, however, which were overcome, so that seven months after the start from Catford those same wheels which had hummed so merrily over the hard, broad road of Kent ground their way through the dust and rubble of Khiva. That Colonel Burnaby had been to Khiva, that twenty-five years before I set out he had established his famous ride, and in the face of all difficulties had accomplished something which no other Englishman had attempted, may be put down as the incentive for my own exploit. Rash and inconsequent it may seem to many—foolhardy to the last degree was what people called it before I started. Even from Russia itself, from people who knew a little of the country I should have to pass through, letters came, urging in most emphatic language the abandonment of a project which was little short of insane.

But I had not started out in the happy-go-lucky manner that many people imagined. For several months before the auspicious day on which I was to bid adieu to England I had assiduously studied the character of my undertaking. The result was that before the last particles of British dust had been shaken from my wheels I knew almost as much of the countries I was to go into, and the manners and customs of their peoples, as those who, being nearer to the spot, had some right to speak with authority. Of course I refer to those lands beyond the Asiatic border, comprising the Khirghiz Steppe, the Kara-kum and Kizil-kum deserts, of Russian Turkestan.

The impossibility of riding the bicycle every inch of the way to Khiva was patent to me before I started. So far as Europe and a goodly portion of Asia were concerned, there was little doubt that the bicycle could be employed to advantage. But there was that stretch of country a thousand miles across the plain of Turkestan, the trackless, waterless waste between Fort No. 1 and the banks of the Oxus River, a dangerous stretch, where I should be compelled to go under escort; while the deep sands of portions of the Kizil-kum desert would make cycling almost, if not quite, an impossibility. All this I realised, but it was to be my endeavour to ride the bicycle as far as it was possible, and the result did not turn out so badly after all, for out of the whole journey of nearly six thousand miles I calculate that less than a hundred were accomplished by any other means than that which the machine afforded.

The cycling papers had already advertised my project to some extent, with the result that a considerable number of cyclists, well known in the sport and pastime, elected to accompany me as far as the coast. Several of these had come from remote parts of London in order to be present at the ceremony of getting away, while some most solemnly asserted that they came to

THE START FROM CATFORD

EN ROUTE TO CALAIS

say good-bye for what they considered to be the last time. On any expedition one is bound to meet with a Job's comforter, and, therefore, I did not feel particularly thankful to the gentleman I met in Riverhead, who, having got wind of my intention, shook my hand with fervour and said, "You will never return!" The labourer in the town of Ashford was more optimistic and more practically British. By some manner of means Ashford had conceived the idea that in my passing through their town they would be treated to a sight equal in its pageantry to that of a circus. The enterprising proprietor of the C.T.C. hotel had caused it to be blazoned forth in all the importance of black-letter type that I should pass through Ashford in the afternoon. Therefore the street of Ashford was crowded. The band of dusty wheelmen in the coffee-room was continuously interrupted in the consumption of its well-earned tea by deputations from the local residents. When a horny-handed son of agricultural toil came in and suggested right off that the people of Ashford would see that I was done right by, even to the extent of raising a subscription should at any portion of the ride my cash run out, I began to think that after all riding a bicycle even on such an insane expedition had compensating advantages.

For the first day a spin of eighty miles was no light task, considering that the season was yet early, the roads were extremely hilly, and so far as regards myself, I was trundling a bicycle weighted up with baggage until it tipped the beam at over sixty pounds. But Dover was reached at last, after an eerie ride over an unknown road from Folkestone. Dover already knew of my intention. The local reporter turned up full of good wishes for my project, and full of solicitations for copy. The local photographer begged permission to take a few snap-shots on the morrow, when I should board one of the Calais boats *en route* to the Continent. A convivial evening with my cycling friends, many promises in the matter of projected correspondence, bed-time, and then the sun shining brilliantly through the window to announce the last day on English soil.

Down on the Admiralty Pier a little crowd

had collected to bid me *bon voyage*. The local correspondent and the local photographer did their fell work. I was introduced to Captain "This" and Captain "That," salts of the first water who had crossed the Channel more times than they could conveniently reckon. Then there was the bundling of the bicycle aboard, the arrival of the trains from London, the scurry and bustle of the people embarking, until at length the siren snorted, people waved handkerchiefs, and the *Empress* cast loose.

I had with me an old clubfellow who intended accompanying me as far as Dunkerque. Arrived at Calais, and once through the Customs, we made haste to consume a modest *déjeuner*, and then set our faces to the east. A rough wind blew steadily against us; a flat, bleak, and un-interesting country stretched to our right and left. Villainous roads were encountered from the very start, a drizzle had fallen, and though in England the sun had been shining brilliantly, here in France the sky was overcast and sombre. Through Gravelines and so on to Dunkerque. Night came down before we reached the maritime town, and here I was to say good-bye to my companion, for business demanded his presence in the square mile of London city on the following day. I saw him off by train, and then wandered out into the streets of fishy, dirty, and smelly Dunkerque until the time came that I sought repose.

On the next day I was up early, gratified at a change in the weather, to find a pleasant breeze blowing on my back and a hard white road to lead me to the Belgian frontier. It was my intention to reach Yprès that day, and, favoured by both road and wind, this was by no means an improbable task. Little indeed was there of interest in my surroundings. Straight roads led me through a country essentially agricultural, with irrigating ditches and steely canals in every direction, lines of gaunt poplars fading away into space, passing now and again some lumbering, oxen-drawn waggon, or some saboted peasant trudging.

Bergues was passed, and at the village of Rexvoode I took my midday repast preparatory to crossing the Belgian frontier. Therefore late in the afternoon I wheeled from French to Belgian soil. Sentries blocked my way and took me courteously to the custom-house. The *douanier* had heard of me, he said, for he was himself a cyclist, and with many smiles produced a copy of a Belgian cycling paper detailing my project. But duty was duty, he said, with a smile and a shake of his head. He wrote a description of my bicycle, he demanded certain moneys for the cycle tax, his assistant affixed a leaden seal to the framework, and then I was free to go.

"Belgian *pavé* is bad," said the *douanier*, "and if it rains don't ride." He winked. "There are plenty of trains in Belgium."

CHAPTER II.

ON BELGIAN *PAVÉ*

BELGIAN *pavé* is very hard, nobbly, and unsentimental. The name of its inventor is unknown, but he is dead now, which for him is most fortunate, since the combined wrath of the world's cyclists would wither him instanter.

This Belgium is a queer little country; I hardly know what to think of it. Sometimes it reminds me of Holland, sometimes of Germany, sometimes of France, and frequently of England, or that part of it adjacent to Dudley, Wednesbury, Walsall, Wolverhampton, and Gornal. Its people are picturesque, industrious, and hospitable; they use more dogs as beasts of draught and burden than horses, speak a language that defies comparison, and look happy. The northern part of the country is flat and uninteresting, and here the men of Flanders gather in their force. Quaint old towns and villages are to be passed through, where the Flemish and French languages get mixed up in indescribable confusion, and where the discomforts of the *pavé* are followed by a long search for someone to understand you.

One day I got into a small Flemish village, and espying the legend "*café*," made for it, and tried both German and French upon an interesting old lady in my desire to obtain a glass of milk. Nothing came of it, until in disgust I blurted out in English, "Oh, give me a glass of milk."

Wonders will never cease, for, although I had spoken in English, I had also spoken in Flemish at one and the same time. The old dame understood me, and I got my milk.

At another place I paused for a little rest, and in a small *café*, which was one of the inns of the Touring Club de Belgique, watched an interesting ceremony. A local cyclist came in with a tyre badly punctured.

The inn was kept by a damsel, fair, fat, and perhaps thirty. She was a vigorous specimen of womanhood, and the way she seized that bicycle, turned it upside down, and whipped off the outer

cover of the tyre was a sight which made me
blink.

The owner of the bicycle stood by doing
nothing, but milady, talking with great volubility
all the time, in that language which seems altogether too impossible, worked like a Trojan at
the repairing tackle.

The sight was so good that I took out my
kodak instanter, prepared to take a picture, but
the damsel, perceiving my object, refused to be
photographed under any circumstances—least of
all in such a costume and at such labour. But
arguments prevailed, and on condition that I
would send a photograph to her the snap-shot
was taken.

Wheeling along the great high roads one over-
takes or meets numbers of queer little dog-carts.
It is astonishing how strong the Belgian dog is.
I have seen quite a heavy vehicle, loaded up with
milk-cans, and perhaps thirty stone of man and
woman, being drawn at quite a smart pace by a
dog which looked neither big nor strong enough
to tackle a healthy rat. Poor brutes, they are
tame enough, and as I swish by them they do

not resent my presence as do the canines of other countries. But there is another dog. He is what I call the "free dog"; the dog that has, for some reason or other, not been called upon to labour. He is very healthy and frisky, comes for me with great gusto, and seems very proud of his dental organisation. I have come prepared for him, however, and the whip I carry serves excellently. Sometimes I miss my canine friend, but when I do not the result is most satisfactory to my feelings.

There is one thing about Belgian roads which I think it is most important to tell. King Leopold has long been an enthusiastic cyclist. He was one of the first to realise how bad for cycling were the paved roads of his country, and in consequence of this the order has gone forth to prepare, on one side of each highway throughout the kingdom, a special cinder track for the exclusive use of cyclists. There is such a track on the road between Yprès and Brussels, and it affords excellent going. I understand that in due time all the roads in Belgium will be provided with cyclists' tracks.

Much of this has been brought about by the energetic action of the Touring Club de Belgique —a model organisation, formed and carried on on the lines of the Touring Club de France. Belgian roads are very badly marked, but the Touring Club has done much to forward this work.

It was night when I arrived in Brussels. The small Paris, as the people call it, and well they might, for with its handsome boulevards, its life, bustle, gaiety, its fine buildings and splendid drives, it vies with the gay city. At night, when the electric sheen plays over the boulevards, one might well imagine himself in Paris, only that the average Belgian is a shade more phlegmatic than the Frenchman, and you hear now and then the guttural voice of the German to remind you that you are not in France.

South-east of Brussels I have fair roads, except when I drop suddenly upon that terrible *pavé;* but the country is bleak and uninteresting. Late on the first day out of the capital I espy in the near distance the outlines of blue hills ahead. Then the road declines rapidly, and of a sudden

I come to a macadamised road, and pedal through clustering trees and by roaring cascades and brawling rivulets, right to the valley of the Meuse.

This is the first glimpse of the Ardennes, that splendid country which saves Belgium from the reproach of being uninteresting. Namur is reached, a tiny town nestling in a valley and by the placid river; around it the thickly wooded hills, and itself a jumble of old houses and tortuous streets.

And now I wheel by the banks of the Meuse, which reminds me here and there of the Moselle, and sometimes of the Rhine, for ruined castles crown the hilltops and frown upon the valley, recalling legends of ancient days when ye lordly robber descended to exact tax from the traveller.

Later on these wooded heights give place to factories and chimneys. I am entering upon the industrial portion of Belgium by Liège. The thump, thump of the steam hammer, the hoarse roar and rattle of machinery, the screech of whistles, the blare of forges and blasts come to my ear as I pedal along. My eyes and throat are choked with coal-dust and cement, the roadway is deep in black cinders and dust, men with oily clothes and grimy faces are seen to right and to left, and I am in Wolverhampton; no, in Liège!

On the following day I was to wheel into the Fatherland, a few kilometres separating me from the frontier, beyond which the land of the Kaiser spread its welcoming arms. My last day in Belgium was well spent, for I was attended by M. Robert Protin, the celebrated champion, and the members of the Liège Cycling Club.

They were earnest in desiring me to stay yet one more day, but I was anxious to sight those black and white posts of the German frontier, to get my forty-eight francs back from the Belgian Government, and to discover whether my friend the Deutscher has forgotten how to make sausages or brew lager beer.

COLOGNE

FRANKFORT-ON-MAIN

CHAPTER III.

ON THE BANKS OF THE RHINE

WHEN Byron went into such raptures over the beauties of the Rhine he did not anticipate the coming of Mr. Cook, or of the tourist, English and American, chaperoned by Mr. Cook; nor did he in his calmest moments imagine what the banks of the Rhine would be like now.

Byron saw only that noble river flowing between massive and impressive hills; he saw only those castellated heights, every peak, every scarp hoary with romance and history. He saw not the desirable hotels, the numerous wine and beer gardens, the steamboats and the tourists' touts. Had he done so he would probably have paused in reflection and might never have written a word about the Rhine.

Still, all the hotels, the villas, the railways,

C 17

tramways, electric lights, steamboats, tugs, barges, tourists, touts, and itinerant troubadours in the world cannot alter, though they may mar, the splendid beauty of the Rhine banks. To wheel beside that classic stream, as I have done, to watch the river broadening and narrowing, to see on every hand great heights uprising, where on the sides vineyards spread in alternating colours, and where hill-peaks are crowned with the crumbling ruins of the castles of the bold Rhenish barons; to see all this is enough, and we can forgive the garish obtrusiveness of the modern.

I struck the Rhine at Cologne, the city of scent, where eau de Cologne is dearer than in London, where spires of a splendid cathedral seem to pierce the blue, and where in odd, out-of-the-way corners one finds many traces of old Prussian life—such as it must have been before there was a German Empire. But Cologne is not new to me; I was here at the time of the world's championships in 1895, and nothing has been altered.

I sat in the same seat of the Café Bauer, in

the Hohe Strasse, where three years previously
I sat surrounded by the *élite* of the world's cyclists,
at a time when that *café* was a babel of French,
German, English, Dutch, Danish—every European
tongue one can think of. The waiter remembers
the world's championships, and the men who
came to win them, and vividly recollects the noise
they made and the glasses they broke. But he
is a man of a kindly disposition, and bears no
malice.

From Cologne to Coblentz is a matter of some
sixty-five miles. There are *chaussées* or high-
ways on both sides of the river, but the best is
that on the left or west side, following as it does
the course of the river the whole way. To get
out of Cologne is not easy, for there is a plenitude
of traffic, both pedestrian and vehicular, while
tramlines and bad setts warn one to be careful.
Once outside the city the way is fair enough to
Bonn, but over a flat and uninteresting country.
Tiny villages, scrupulously clean, with houses
built in the old German style, are passed through,
and after Bonn one sees right ahead the blue outlines of the heights of the Drachenfels.

The sun is hot and the south-east wind blows dead on the handle-bar. It is collar work against the blast, and at Rolandseck I am constrained to cross the river to Unkel in order to obtain the shelter of the hills. Now the banks of the Rhine assume a grand aspect.

The hills get higher and higher and more picturesque, ruined castles are more frequent, and the villages more ancient and quaint. Through Erpel, Linz, and Rheinbrol, sheltered as I am from the wind, the going is fine, and I strike company with a German cyclist who is bound for Coblentz, a cyclist who knows his Rhine and appreciates its wine.

Rhine wine! There used to be a lusty song in England, the refrain of which was one long exhortation to let the Rhine wine flow. Well, it flows fast enough on the banks of the river: clear amber, and twopence a tumbler; or if you are fastidious you can have a bottle of the best for sixpence. German beer is at a discount; it is altogether not to be thought of in the land of wine.

The railway porter smokes his cigar and drinks

wine (which would cost six or more shillings a bottle in England) with a nonchalance born of custom and experience. In the small inns where we stop occasionally, it is a sight to see the peasants living, as it would seem, in the lap of luxury, for here is a land apparently overflowing with the riches of nature.

At Neuweid the river is once more crossed, and a fast run to Coblentz made. Off to the left the fortress of Ehrenbreitstein stands grim and formidable amongst the rocks. Ahead the river narrows, and off to the right the mouth of the Moselle opens to discharge its waters into the Rhine.

The best part of the Rhine is undoubtedly that between Coblentz and Bingen. The river is narrower, and rushes along at a tremendous pace. The heights are more rugged and savage, and ruined castles more numerous. The road, too, is magnificent, with a surface which would equal that of any racing track, and it is easy to attain a good pace, though that would be sacrilege, since to hurry through such scenery is not to be thought of.

Passing through small villages, little children come running out, shouting in their shrill treble, "All heil! Radfahrer, all heil!" Anon some frisky dog will frolic about the pedals—to get a touch of whip-thong across his snout. One passes some lumbering waggon drawn by sleek and patient oxen, or some small dogcart in which sits mein herr, phlegmatic and fat, pipe in mouth, and contented with all the world.

Bingen at last, and here the river turns abruptly to the east to join the Main at Mainz.

We have all heard of Bingen-on-the-Rhine; poets and writers have all gone into ecstasies over it; but I don't.

Why? Because it is raining hard, and, if one can judge from the appearance of the skies, it is going to continue to rain hard—the streets are swimming in water, a grey haze spreads over the hilltops facing the window of my hotel, and I am gloomy because Frankfort, which I desire to make my destination for the day, is only fifty kilometres further on.

CHAPTER IV.

ON THE BAVARIAN HILLS

THE *ober-kellner* at the hotel in Frankfort-on-Main was lucid in his directions. "It is about two hours," said he, "from here to the Bavarian border. Don't forget what I have told you: be careful in that country, for the Bavarians are pigs."

This and much more was told me; that the hills of Bavaria were frightfully steep, that the roads were bad, that the people were miserable, that the food was scarce and the beer was poor. Beer touches the German more than anything else; give him good beer and he is happy, give him bad and he is indeed a wretched man; and yet we learn, or are told, that Munich is in Bavaria, and from Munich comes the finest lager. Strange that the Prussian should think otherwise.

The roads were fair enough to the border,

23

although a blustering wind made the going heavy. Hills there were, but not steep enough to render them unrideable to my 56-inch gear. At the border, good-bye to the Prussian Eagle, and "all heil!" to the two lions of the Bavarian king. The black and white posts of Prussia give way to the blue and white of this conservative country; everything is new, interesting. Houses take a new shape, people a different costume, peasants speak a patois. German stamps and postcards are no good here, one must needs have those of Bavaria—and yet this Bavaria is Germany, sworn to the German Kaiser, and bound to fight for Germany. But Bavaria is Germany since 1866 only, and the period subsequent to that year has had very little effect in altering Bavarian character.

I reached Aschaffenburg on the first day, and the weather had set in terrifically hot. Here I chummed in with a German cyclist who was making his way by easy stages to Nuremburg. It appeared that this handsome and gallant son of the Fatherland had a sweetheart in Bavaria's oldest city, and periodically, three times a year, made a pilgrimage from his native Cologne to

the shrine of his love. Since I was alone in
Bavaria I was glad, indeed, of his company, and
we got on merrily together.

Aschaffenburg to Wurzburg, a distance of only
forty miles, took us all day—and no wonder when
we take into account the hills, nay, mountains,
which we were compelled to climb. I do not
want to pose as a grumbler, for the compensating feature of those hills was the grand panorama
of country everywhere obtainable. Think of it! a
five kilometres alternative walk and ride to the
top of a hill, and to pause there, and seated on
some grassy knoll, watch the glorious scene below.
The hills tumbled one upon another, the streaks
of stream glittering here and there like ribands
of silver; a cluster of white and red houses shining
in the sunlight; patches of agriculture alternately
red, brown, and green; terraces of vines; all making up a picture never to be forgotten.

At a small village, soon after Aschaffenburg,
we paused to drink a litre of beer at an inn,
and there fell in with a party of hunters who were
making their midday meal. Picturesque fellows
are these Bavarian jagers, with their green

costumes, knee breeches, and comical little hats and feathers. A merry party they made, and invited us to accompany them into the neighbouring forest to hunt the wild swine—or, to put it in English, the boar. Never having had the opportunity of seeing the boar in his native forest, I fell in with the suggestion gladly, and so we set out.

It was an interesting procession. First went a swarthy fellow called Hans, carrying on his shoulder a small keg of beer (for how could the Bavarian hunt without beer?). Hans had in his mouth a pipe three feet long, which possessed a china bowl of wondrous beauty. Fritz, who followed him, carried a couple of guns and the hunting knives. He also possessed three feet of pipe. Then came the others, half a dozen in all, every man armed to the teeth, but a jovial crowd as ever was. A tramp of a mile or so over a by-path in the forest and then we plunged into the depths of the wood. Here, where the trees were so thick and the undergrowth so dense that we had to fairly force a passage, the change from the open was astonishing. The bright, blue sky and the golden sun were completely obscured, and everything was as in a gloaming. Quietness reigned supreme, broken only by the faint "chirp-chirp" of some bird in the branches of the trees above, the patter of some squirrel as he hastily fled for shelter, the drone of innumerable insects, or the scattering sound of the dead leaves as we forced our way through the brambles.

It was tiring work, and after an hour of it a halt was called, and the beer keg was broached. A litre around, and then preparations were made to find the pigs. They were somewhere in the neighbourhood, but I found that, like the Siberian bear, they are timid, and want forcing to fight. Our party scattered, disappearing as if by magic amongst the trees. I kept close to Hans, the leader of the party, and for ten minutes or more we scrunched steadily through the thicket. Presently there rang out in mournful clearness the notes of a hunting horn, followed immediately by the crack of a rifle.

Then quietness for a moment, then the blast of the horn again. We came out into a small, open space, and on the other side caught a glimpse of a couple of jagers as they moved among the trees. Bang! went a rifle, and bang! bang! bang! in quick succession three more reports. Out of the thicket there darted at terrific speed an ungainly-looking object which looked like nothing so much as a small bear covered with thick hair, its long snout projecting straight out from the huge hump on its shoulders, and its white teeth showing. It looked indeed a formidable object.

It headed straight for where we were standing, and the squealings and gruntings it gave voice to were hair-raising in their intensity. My instinct was to turn and make a bolt for it, but the shock of an explosion at my side brought me to, and I saw the pig on its side, squealing fearfully, but mortally shot. A quarter of an hour afterwards I saw a sight which was worth going a long way to see. Fifty or more sows, followed by their young, tearing and crashing through the undergrowth, creating a fearful din as they careered along. The jagers do not hunt the sows, but reserve their fire for the old man of the forest, but he is a difficult customer to catch and often a dangerous antagonist.

This hunting of wild animals is keen sport, and no wonder the Bavarian jager, who hunts the chamois and the wild deer in the Tyrol, or the bear and boar in the forest, looks with contempt upon the sport of bird shooting or rabbit catching. Late in the afternoon we bade good-bye to our merry and kindly hosts. A litre of beer from the keg, guttural "Prosits!" "Good luck!" and "Good journey!" and then making our way back to the inn we resumed our bicycles and our way.

There is little incident for me to chronicle in my journey over the mountains to Nuremburg— Bavaria's ancient and historical city. It is true I am wheeling in a country but little known to the British cycling tourist. Indeed, it is evident from the way horses shy and dogs bark and snarl at the sight of my bicycle that cycling altogether is not of very great proportions in the outlying districts.

As I progress further eastward, every day's ride serves to show some change from the Occident, a gradual merging of the Teuton with the Slav. The sprightly, clean, and even dainty German villages give place to squalid hamlets. Children and women go barefoot; oxen are the principal means of draught. The inns are rather dirty and evil smelling, and the people of saturnine aspect. Still I am kindly treated, and when I rest and answer the innumerable questions put to me by good-natured Bavarians the interest taken in me is intense.

Sometimes it is amusing to watch the effect produced by the announcement that I have ridden a bicycle from England. The "Ach Himmel!" or the "Donnerwetter!" of surprise, or the look of incredulity or unfeigned "well-you-must-be-a-liar" sort of expression which comes over their bronzed countenances!

I stayed over a day in Nuremburg in order to see one or two of the sights of this noble old town, and then off again, heading towards the Austrian frontier, now less than 200 miles away; hills upon hills, with the road winding through the valleys or climbing in gigantic zigzags the ponderous slopes.

Nuremburg is left behind, and one day late in the afternoon I come out on the ridge of the hills, and see below me a wide, spreading valley. Away ahead I perceive the sheen of water—a broad river flowing eastward in silent majesty.

It is the Danube!

CHAPTER V.

BY THE BLUE DANUBE

THE blue Danube was decidedly yellow when first I saw it. Still, one mustn't be too hard or too cynical, for have we not our own silvery Thames? And if the Danube was muddy at Ratisbon, so is old Father Thames everywhere, except above Reading.

But here it was, the Danube at last, whose course I was to follow as far as Buda-Pest, whence, while the river went south to flow through fair Roumania, and past the bloody battlefields made by the Russo-Turkish war, I should go north-east into the land of the Carpathians.

On Sunday morning, to the chiming of the bells of Ratisbon, I pedalled out once more into the country. Off to my left the fast-flowing river ran its course. Ahead of me stretched a flat and sterile-looking land, although, in the dim distance, the rugged outlines of the hills of the Austrian Oberland showed clear and distinct. The road was fair enough, and with the wind behind I had no difficulty in making Straubing in good time. But the wind, though kind, brought misfortune. Clouds scurried across the sky. The "blue" Danube, yellower than ever, raced and seethed along in veritable ocean waves. Rain fell, and at Straubing I was house-bound.

A black and gloomy sky, a moaning wind, and streets swimming in rain-water! That was the outlook when I pulled out for the Austrian frontier next morning. It was work indeed to push my machine through the sodden clay and sand which formed the roadway. Everything looked bleak and deserted; and as I splashed through some village there would be no sign of life, unless it were a brood of geese muddling by the roadside, or some mire-caked pig grunt-ing and nosing through the ooze. Dogs would yelp occasionally, and make futile efforts to get at me, but the mud would be too much.

D

Sometimes I caught a glimpse of a peasant sheltering beneath the overhanging eaves of his cottage, diligently smoking his pipe, and regarding me, as I splurged along, with a look of stolid wonderment. Out in the country I would perchance overtake a rumbling waggon, the heavy oxen steaming and straining at their laborious task, the driver enveloped in sacks, and ever smoking. Sometimes I would pass a benighted Bavarian tramp, who, with shoes slung over shoulder, and whose jaunty green cap looked sadly bedraggled, slouched miserably along. The drizzle of the morning became in the afternoon a perfect downpour. In a tiny and squalid village I sought shelter, and in sheer disgust abandoned the idea of getting to Passau that night.

Bavarian villages may never be noted for being up to date. This one in particular was a mere collection of brick and timber huts, standing now in a sea of mud. There was a *gasthof* of diminutive proportions, in the one room of which twenty or more rain and beer-soaked peasants were indulging in a carousal. They stared askance at me as I entered, my mud-covered mackintoshes streaming.

The reek of Bavarian tobacco, the all-pervading smell of Bavarian beer, the humid odour of un-washed Bavarian clothing caused me to gasp. Friendly but blear-eyed men came to me with their mugs that I might refresh myself. The proprietor generously pushed an old man out of his seat in order that I might have a place. A foaming mug of beer was placed before me, and I had received a Bavarian welcome—all they had to give. Rough, uncouth, unwashed, yet kind, these Bavarians are not bad fellows to a stranger. "Money I haven't got," says the child of the Danube bank, "but everything else is for you."

An accordion with one or two leaky notes squeaked out a monstrous melody, and a heavy peasant flopped into the middle of the room to give us a sight of his Terpsichorean capabilities; round and round he wheeled to the admiration of the onlookers. The room was thick with smoke, hot and stifling. Once I went to the door to get a breath of fresh air, and to note with chagrin the persistently descending rain, the scurrying clouds, and the mist on the hill-tops ahead.

The afternoon was waning when, rain or no rain, I set out intent on reaching Passau that night. To stop in that village when a lively and bustling town was only twenty miles away was not an agreeable prospect. I couldn't get much wetter, and my poor bicycle was a mere mass of revolving mud.

Night settled down, and the steady downpour became a storm. Lightning darted across the black expanse of the heavens, thunder rolled and boomed. The rain eased now and again, only to return with tropical intensity. Once from the brow of a small hill I caught a glimpse of welcoming lights ahead : the sheen of electric lamps playing on the surging waters of the Danube.

On my right side ran the railway, and five miles from Passau a mail train came thundering along. As it passed I saw, within the brightly-lit carriages, indistinct heads of people reclining in ease and comfort on warm cushions. Then the train was gone in a blaze of sparks and light, and I shivered and jerked heavily at the pedals.

But everything has an end, and an hour later, when in borrowed clothes I was doing justice to an ample dinner and tasting my first Hungarian wine, I became a little happier. I was now on the Austrian frontier, and to-morrow would leave the land of the Deutscher Kaiser for that of Franz Joseph, Emperor of Austria and King of Hungary. Kind friends in Passau told me horrible stories of the inhospitality of Austrians and the barbarous tactics of Hungarians, but I ate much salt with my food and the stories, for I had already learned that race hatred here in the Danubian provinces is deep and lasting.

"When you get to Neuhaus," said the proprietor of the *gasthaus*, "you have got to cross the River Inn by a small bridge. Half of the bridge belongs to Bavaria, and the other half belongs to Austria. In the middle of the bridge is an Austrian customs-house, and there you'll have to pay sixty marks duty on your bicycle— that is, if they catch you. If I were you I'd just get across that bridge as hard as ever I could go, dodge the guard, and there I'd be, and not a penny to pay." Such excellent advice as this was not to be treated lightly. An hour after leaving Passau I came in sight of the River Inn, and at Neuhaus, the last Bavarian town, drank my last glass of German beer.

Even as the proprietor of the Passau hotel had advised, I rode hard up the slope of the Inn bridge, saw, but took no notice of, the blue and white and black and yellow posts of Bavaria and Austria side by side, and with a clear run before me, for the bridge was deserted, put on a spurt, and began to congratulate myself I was all right.

But I reckoned without my host. I heard a hoarse shouting behind me, and as I careered on down the slope of the bridge saw a soldier in the middle of the road waving his arms excitedly. There was no help for it. I jammed on the brake and rode peacefully into custody.

"Donnerwetter!" cried the soldier. "What do you mean by riding past the customs?"

"Donnerwetter!" cried I. "What do you mean by stopping me?"

But Germans don't waste time in argument. The soldier hauled me back to the customs-house, where half a dozen stern and severe officers looked at me as if I were a criminal of the deepest dye. I at once assumed an utter ignorance of the German language, and only smiled when they commenced their tirade of abuse. I spoke to them in English and shrugged my shoulders, produced my passport, and sat down on the kerb.

They gave me up as a bad job at last. An aged functionary affixed a leaden seal to my machine, another one handed me a paper and demanded sixty marks. Sixty marks he got, and I was bidden to " be off." It is evident that dodging the customs does not command respect.

And I was in Austria! A land built up of ten nationalities, where race pride and race hatred are more rampant than in any other corner of the earth. A fair enough land for him who comes unbiassed and unprejudiced; and such was I, for I cared little for the internal strife between Bohemian, German, Pole, Hungarian, Crotian, Slavonian, Bosnian, and all the rest of them who go to make up Austria. Hills there were ahead of me, which I should have to cross, and these commanded all my attention for the nonce.

Politics were for those who made them; for me
the country was simply as it impressed me.

My first two days in Austria were pleasant
enough. Improved weather made the going easy,
and I passed Linz, Melk, St. Polten, and came
within measurable distance of the city of Vienna.
Only one incident served to give colour and
romance to my ride, one of those incidents
which might occur even in England, but which far
away from the old country always wear a more
serious aspect. Now and again some enthusiastic
local cyclist would turn out to give me a lead.
I should be a curmudgeon to look a gift-horse
in the mouth, but sometimes I have wished that
some of the local cyclists would not turn out at
all. Some fifty miles or so west of Vienna I struck
a small village, and while consuming a humble
repast in burst a perspiring cyclist, who immediately made known to me that he intended
to accompany me for twenty kilometres.

He was a good sort, but rode a German-made
racing machine, with a gear approaching a hundred
inches. He criticised my mount severely, and
could not understand how on earth I should

AMONGST THE HUNGARIAN CYCLISTS

have selected such a heavy bicycle for my ride instead of having a racer.

The road out of the village was hilly and terribly loose. For five kilometres the course wound round and round, but ever upwards. At length we came to the top, and saw below the smiling valley of the Danube and the great rolling hills beyond. Now the way descended abruptly, and we went spinning down at a spanking pace, the wheels crashing and skittering through the rubble and loose stones which bestrewed the surface. My companion was leading me by about five or six yards, when, with a suddenness which was hair-raising, his machine crumpled up like a piece of paper and he went flying through the air.

Another moment and I should have been foul of the wreck, but instinct caused me to wrench round my handle-bar. The back wheel skidded in the loose stuff; I missed the wreck by bare inches, bounded up the embankment on the side of the road, struck against a telegraph post, and went head over heels four feet below into a dry ditch, with my machine on top of me.

For a moment I thought the bicycle must be

smashed. I was up instantly, and my joy was great to find that nothing was broken. I climbed out of the ditch and saw my companion sitting in the middle of the road surveying with sorrowful eyes the jumbled-up mass of metal and rubber which represented his racer. Poor fellow, he was sad enough. I went on to the next village and sent a cart out to fetch him and his broken machine, and that done, pursued the even tenor of my way, more than ever determined not to ride too near a German-built racer in future.

Nearing Vienna the roads became miserable in the extreme. For the last ten miles they were quite unrideable, and I was forced to foot it. Tramping is slow work, however, and I took to the footpath, which made decent running. I was three miles from Vienna when a policeman hauled me off and inquired, politely, at any rate, what I had got to say for myself.

"I didn't know it was forbidden to ride on the footpath," said I, with a stare of blank astonishment. "I am a foreigner, and you haven't any notice boards saying it is prohibited to ride here."

"You are a foreigner, yes, and you look like an

intelligent man, and an intelligent man should know that it is forbidden to ride bicycles on the footpath anywhere. Yes, that is the way to Vienna. Please don't do it again."

I accepted the rebuff, trudged steadily through the sand of the roadway, and an hour later was in the whirl of the traffic of Austria's capital.

CHAPTER VI.

IN THE LAND OF THE UNGARN

"Wenn Menschen auseinandergeh'n
Dann sagen sie: Auf Wiederseh'n."

"AT the next village," said Adalbert Szalay, of the Vienna Bicycle Club, "we shall pass into Hungary. This hill on your right is Austrian, that on your left is Hungarian. See! there is the post—green, white, red!" He raised his cap even as he spoke, for he was a true Hungarian, and he was happy to be once more on the soil of his fatherland.

From Vienna to the Hungarian border the way had been fair enough. True, the surface of the military *chaussée* would not compare for one moment with the turnpikes of England, but one must not cavil when there are roads at all to ride upon, and, come good or bad surface, one should thank his stars that the machine remains upright.

44

Out of Vienna seven or eight enthusiasts had formed my escort, and the destination for the day —Pressburg—was over the Hungarian border. Visions of the Tzigané, those celebrated Hungarian gipsies, came before my eyes as our wheels rumbled through the dust into the land of the Magyar.

Off to the left on the crown of a hill a square, solid castle frowned down upon the waters of the Danube. It marked the site of Pressburg, once the stronghold of the Hungarians. Beneath the castle, and nestling on the banks of the river, was the pretty town itself, embedded, it appeared, in a wealth of lilac and laburnum. Over the high iron bridge, and along a shaded boulevard, and here we are at last, really in Hungary.

To write of the land of the Magyar and not to mention the Tzigané would be like attempting to write about Egypt and never suggest the word "backsheesh." Hungary is Austrian, so says the Austrian; but the Hungarian is patriotic enough to repudiate the suggestion. For political motives Hungary is part of Austria; for every other reason it is distinctly anti-German. There is a

different money, different postage stamp, different
flag, different language—everything different, in
short. It would seem as if the Hungarian tried
his level best to make his country as great a
contrast as possible with that of the king to whom
he owes allegiance. At any rate, says the Hungarian, the Austrians have no Tzigané, and he
is right.

Wheeling through this fair country with the
blue hills of the Little Carpathians off to my left,
with the Danube showing here and there, over fair
roads, by vineyards and stretches of prim agriculture, is pleasant enough work. One day I
came upon a band of gipsies, swarthy vagabonds,
speaking an unintelligible patois, and as picturesque as you please. What matters that the
men were so ragged that their scanty clothing
hung in ribbons, that the women in short skirts
and decked out in beads and gewgaws howled
with laughter at my costume, that the children
went stark naked? These were the originals of
all the zingari of the world.

From Pressburg to Buda-Pest was a two days'
journey. Intelligence had been conveyed to me

that the Buda-Pest cyclists intended to come out on the road to offer a welcome to a wandering Englishman. But there were two roads into Buda-Pest, and at Raab, a quaint Magyar town, I tossed up a kreutzer to decide the way, and rode to Buda-Pest over one of the vilest roads in Christendom.

One hundred and twenty-five kilometres is not much for a day's ride when the road and the wind are fair; but with a road so bad as that between Raab and Pest it was a colossal performance. I started from Raab cheerily enough, a gentle breeze blowing on my back, and with a level, though dusty, road beneath me. At midday, when the sun was doing its best to roast me, I was in a country which for wild uncivilisation was so great a contrast to the country of yesterday as to be striking. Now the road deteriorated alarmingly, miniature bogs and small Saharas of sand were offered to obstruct my progress. Locomotion per bicycle became more and more difficult; when there was not sand there was swamp, or deep cart ruts in gluey clay, or stones as big as a negro's head. The day waned, the sun went down blood red at my back and shot the hills on the northern horizon with a sheen of gold. Ahead the blue-grey mist of evening was creeping like a shroud over a tumbled country—and I was still fifty kilometres from my destination.

Bump! rattle! scrunch! swish! I plunged along steadily, and once from out the wilderness I caught the glint of the sun's last ray on a church spire. It was the church of Biscke village.

Over the brow of a hill and down a long slope, so that, ten minutes later, I was pedalling slowly through the sandy street to the accompaniment of much barking from dogs, hissing from geese, grunting from pigs, quacking from ducks, and unlimited applause from the local human population—to see, in the middle of the road, a cyclist waving his arms excitedly. It was Louis Kiss, whom I last saw on English roads in the days when road racing was rampant, and police magistrates were not nearly so anti-cyclist as now. From the Ripley road to the heart of Hungary is a wide step; and what a reunion!

From Biscke to Pest had to be done in the darkness. It was a wild and eerie ride. Plunging down unknown hills, smashing through stones, clay, and sand. Kiss had telegraphed to Pest that we should arrive at eleven o'clock, and to do so over such roads was no mean task.

Black as a hat came the night, scarcely a yard could one see ahead, and now and again some wayfarer, journeying Heaven knows whither, would bob up in the halo of our lamps to give us a shock, and to disappear silently into the night. Or now and again the rumble of a vehicle would reach our ears, and we would pass some heavy waggon drawn by a yoke of oxen, with the driver, true to his calling, sleeping the sleep of the just.

Twinkling lights appeared in the distance, and a long-drawn cry came floating on the warm air. Brighter and brighter the sparks of light became; the tinkling of bells was heard; shouts and counter shouts; a babel of tongues and echoing cries of "All heil! All heil!" and we rode into a glare thrown by the lamps of twenty-five wheelmen of Buda-Pest, and I was busy with hand-shaking.

E

The road improved now, and the cavalcade grew to unwieldy proportions as the Hungarian capital was approached. Eleven o'clock it was as we rattled over the *pavé* of Buda-Pest, and at 11.2 dismounted outside the club lokal of the Buda-Pest Cyclists' Club, where in the saloon the Tzigané orchestra struck up "God Save the Queen" in honour of my arrival and of my nationality.

To stay long in Buda-Pest would be to engender the desire to stay there a month. Vienna had been suggested to me as the finest city in Austro-Hungary. But my humble opinion gives the palm to Buda-Pest. This historical city, the stronghold of the Turks in the days when the green banner of Islam moved steadily across Europe; through which the blue Danube (yellower than ever) flows and eddies; where the national characteristics of the true Hungarian are best seen; where the civilisation of the nineteenth century deals lightly with old-time association; this city, I repeat, must be visited to be enjoyed.

"As long as you are in Hungary," said the

captain of the club, "you shall have company.
Yes, right to the frontier; and after that"—he
pursed his lips and looked solemn—"after that
there is Galicia, and there you will find the Poles
and Jews, donnerwetter, Jews!"

So on the morning of May 19th I bade farewell
to Buda-Pest, gave my last glance to the Danube,
and headed out for the Carpathians. Flat roads
and a good wind gave promise of decent riding for
the first few days. Herr Bollock, the editor of
the *Hungarian Cyclist*, was to accompany me as
far as the Polish border, and, in addition, I had
an enthusiastic escort for over 100 kilometres.

Fuzes Abony was made on the first day out,
Kaschau on the second, and Eperjes on the
third. Here, in a small town on the foothills of
the Carpathians, with a population of 12,000, was
a bicycle club of noble proportions, the members
of which vied with each other to show me
kindness.

What can I do except acknowledge in cold
print the generous feelings of these Magyar
wheelmen towards a Briton? If I get a swollen
head, lay the blame at the gate of Hungary.

Next day I stood on one of the spurs of the lower Carpathians.   Before me was a wild and tumbled country.   Great mountains piled, it would seem, one upon another.   Jagged masses of rock showing white out of the green of the virgin forest.   Here, on this spur, the green, white, and red post of Hungary stood side by side with the yellow and black post of Austrian Galicia—and here was the Hungarian frontier.   The captain of the Eperjes Bicycle Club was with me.

He shook my hands with fervour.   "Herr Jefferson," said he, "we wish you on your journey all the success you could wish yourself.   Luck and health!   And, perhaps, when you return to your fatherland, and to those who are bound to you, you will think sometimes of the simple Ungarn!"

A VINEYARD INSPECTOR IN OFFICIAL ROBES

CHAPTER VII.

ACROSS THE CARPATHIANS

IT was nine o'clock in the morning, and the little town of Bartfeld, on the Hungarian side of the Carpathians, was hardly astir. True, here and there, one caught a glimpse of the red petticoat of some industrious peasant woman wending her way across the fields to where the great black pines made a forest dark and sombre. The road here was level, but before me loomed the gigantic peaks of the Carpathians. Off to the left the celebrated Tatra heights reared themselves in majesty. Off to the right the undulating slopes of the Ober-Ungarn melted into the horizon, and between these two, by the Dukla pass, I was to wheel my bicycle into Galicia, and further into Austrian Poland.

The road became steeper, and it was hard work pushing at pedals. Now and again one was forced to dismount for a breather, mayhap to rest on a mossy bank and smoke a cigarette, meanwhile to watch the fleecy clouds tipping the cones of the mountains or spreading a mist amongst the hollows of the hills.

But the summit of the first range was reached at last.   Hungary was at my back, Galicia before me, and a gentle slope took me briskly into a smiling valley, where a village, perched on the banks of a rushing stream, was pretty enough to cause me to pause for a little while.   The sun was now making its presence felt, and a burning thirst was the provocative to an inquiry of a wandering native as to the whereabouts of a place where refreshment for man or beast might be obtained.   He was a quaint specimen of humanity, this Galician, with his sheepskin coat and woolly hat.   He stared hard at me for a minute or two, shrugged his shoulders and passed on. The German language was wasted upon him!

But perseverance brings results.   I found a hovel dignified by the name of *gasthaus*.   I fell up the wooden steps and nearly broke my head against the cross-beam of the low doorway.

There was a door on my right, and another on my left. Being right-handed I chose the former, and discovered a female engaged in the interesting pursuit of peeling onions. She was blonde to straw colour, had a sort of sack bodice, skirt to her knees, and revelled in being free from the trammels of stockings or shoes.

" Is it possible," I asked, in my best Unter-den-Linden German, "for a man to have a glass of beer ? "

She stared at me for a moment and then shook her head.

" Beer ! " said I vehemently, " beer ! "

She shook her head again.

And though I asked her twice she did not understand me. What sort of language should I practise ? Beyond my own I knew the smatterings of only three. My miserable French was not to be thought of here in Galicia. German had failed. I tried Russian, and in the staccato tongue of the Muscovite reiterated my inquiries for refreshments.

Wonder of wonders ! The woman understood, and in the place of the look of stupidity which

she wore there came an expression of intelligence.   So here in Austria, a German-speaking
nation, I could only make my wants understood
in the Slavic language.   At any rate I got my
refreshment, I paid my score, departed, and
pushed on towards the mountains.

Ye tourists who annually do your Switzerland!
Ye gentle mountaineers who revel in anecdote
of the Tyrol!   Ye folk who talk of the Hielands
of bonny Scotland, and are never tired, worse
luck, of telling us of them, what would you say,
I wonder, if you were dropped from a balloon
one of these fine days on the western slopes
of the Carpathians, and were asked to go over
them into the land of the Pole?

If you were not *blasé* of travel, I can imagine
what you would do.   You would stand and stare
and gasp at the wonderful beauty of mountain
scenery presented to you.   Here in the Carpathians
are no *pension* hotels.   Guides are conspicuous
by their absence.   Alpenstocks have never been
seen, and, further, the white helmet and the blue
goggles of Britain are strangers to this land of
romance and ideality.

So one could enthuse, but with the sun at its meridian, with the sweat pouring down one's face, with the white dust rising from the wheels, and with all one's strength put forth in pressure upon the pedals, one is apt to be more commonplace.

Sometimes I cursed the hills because they were so very steep, and the roadway so very bad, and I seemed to be ever going upwards. Once I came to the crown of a hill, where the land lay bare and desolate. Away ahead spread the rolling country, closed in by those domes of mountains in terrific grandeur. Not a house to be seen, not a speck speaking of the handiwork of man. Here was nature as it might have been thousands of years ago. This hill of sandstone staring redly from the right, that virgin forest showing blue-green and dark on my left, those tumbled hills, all shapes, all sizes, away ahead ; and here, if I must correct myself, the sinuous road creeping by boulder and cascade and tree, ever, ever onward.

The sun declined and sent its hot rays on my back. I was now descending the eastern slopes. My right hand ached with holding the brake lever, and as I rattled and bumped through the rubble in the roadway, or jerked from side to side when ruts and stones obstructed my progress, I felt interested, though tired. Once I passed through a small mountain village, and the peasants flocked out to see the extraordinary spectacle of a bicycle and a bicyclist in the Carpathians.

Can I blame the dogs that they barked and snapped at my heels, or the geese that hissed defiantly at me, or the peasants themselves, who rolled out guffaws of laughter at what was to them a ludicrous sight?

A teamster, toiling along the road, made way for me, forgot his horses in his interest in my method of locomotion, and as I turned at a bend of the way it was to see him sitting there on his load of stone staring blankly, amazedly after me.

It had been my intention to stay at Zmigrod that night, for with all that mountain climbing fifty miles was enough for one day. Already the sun was setting, and it wanted yet ten miles to Zmigrod. Visions of a comfortable hotel, a good evening meal, a reposeful bed, rose before me, and

IN THE CARPATHIANS

A GALICIAN CONFIRMATION PROCESSION

when at last I saw the white façade of Zmigrod's church blinking out of the dark background of fir, pine, and beech I felt happy. The foothills now became less tiresome, and soon I reached the outskirts of the town.

The first man I met was a Jew. He wore a long gabardine reaching to his heels. He was muffled up to his neck, and on his head was perched a big fur cap, with the hair projecting longitudinally. On each side of his face he wore long ringlets reaching almost to his shoulder. He stared at me from a pair of deep sunken black eyes. His face was sallow; his lips coarse; his whole personality hideous.

The second man I met was his brother, the third, the fourth, the fifth—and I rolled into the town. A town of Galician Jews, all attired in similar garments, all patrolling the streets. And the town stunk. The rotten edifices on either side of the only street were of wood, and literally falling to pieces.

Mud lay deep on the roadway. Offal and more noisome refuse were to the right, the left, everywhere. I was forced to dismount, and instantly

I was surrounded by a crowd of evil-smelling Hebrews.

"The best hotel in the place?" said I.

A dozen hands were pulling at my coat. I freed myself with a jerk, and resented the interference of a dirty vagabond, who would ring my bicycle bell, by a kick on the shin.

"The best hotel in the place—where is it?"

"This way, this way," from a chorus of voices.

Then they led me into a hovel of wood and mud, and with eyes blinking and brilliant with avarice showed me the room they desired me to sleep in. "Only two florins, Mein Herr, only two florins."

I was choked with the stench of the place. I looked partly with loathing and partly with fear upon that mass of Jewish faces which surrounded me, and then, unable to control my disgust, I burst from them, forced my way through them, and ran my machine down into the road.

A hop, skip, and a jump, and I was in the saddle. I caught the pedal and pushed ahead. I rang my bell and slashed my whip. So great was the temper of my disgust at this fetid hole, that I rode blindly at every Jew who opposed my passage, and caused him to scatter unceremoniously.

Then I was out of the town, and by the light of a match consulted my map. Dukla was fifteen miles away, but, according to the map, was a tolerably large town. "If I rode all night I would reach it," was my thought. "If I lost my way in the darkness I would sleep on the wayside."

The stars came out and the crescent of the new moon shed a pale light on my way. I pushed on steadily, walking now and again when the road was bad. Ten o'clock came, and soon after I saw the reflected lights of a town before me.

And when I rode into it the first man I met was a Jew, the counterpart of the first man in Zmigrod, and the second, the third, the fourth—everybody, it seemed. I was in despair, for the hour was late; I was tired, hungry. But I found an hotel at last. Hotel! May a Christian never see a worse.

They showed me a room for one florin, and in it were half a dozen Jews, smoking furiously. "But they can go into another room," said the Hebrew proprietor, "and then you can sleep."

His grin and his blackened teeth almost made me sick.

I asked for the best room in the place, cost what it might. They gave me a room on the first floor, big enough for a ball-room, but with a bed little bigger than a cradle; there were two chairs and a table; cobwebs hung in the corners; and the price was five shillings and sixpence.

That night I put my safety catch on the door, and for the first time since leaving England unwrapped my revolver and carefully placed five leaden messengers in its accommodating chambers.

CHAPTER VIII.

AMONGST THE GALICIANS

I PULLED out early from Dukla, the seductive comforts of a Jewish bed and Jewish hospitality notwithstanding. I paid the exorbitant bill without a wink, and accepted the grinning wishes for a safe journey from mine host for what they were worth. I slipped out of town before its gabardined inhabitants were well astir, climbed the short, stiff hill that led to the uplands, and there opened my lungs to take in the fresh, pure air of heaven.

Before me the rolling country spread away to the horizon, and fifty-six miles separated me from Premysal, where I hoped to get that day. Fifty-six miles is but a bagatelle for a cyclist, fit and well, to make on the fair roads of England, but here, in Galicia, it is no mean task.

Up and down, down and up, went the road.

Short, stiff slopes that required a deal of pushing at, and sometimes walking. Descents so abrupt that my hand ached with holding the brake rod. It was impossible to coast, for the benevolent Austrian Government makes not its roads for cyclists, and at every fifty yards or so a deep gully intersects the roadway, over which one must pass carefully or smash one's wheel.

It was easy to see that I was now in a country distinctly removed in every characteristic from that of the Hungarian. The villages through which I passed were mere collections of mud hovels. The people were dark, saturnine, and ostentatiously insulting. Sullen men and women stood in the roadway, and refused to move at the tinkle of my bell. Only when the chance of collision was imminent would they deign to step a trifle on one side and allow me to squeeze by, and when I spoke they snarled.

It was even so with the teamsters; worse, perhaps, as the sequel shows. These teamsters were almost all of Moldavian character. Short, ugly men, wearing an extraordinary costume and a peculiar peaked hat, like nothing so much as a naval captain's full dress hat. They drove small, spirited horses, and were prone to occupy the whole of the road.

Time after time was I compelled to hurriedly dismount and plunge into the ditch to avoid being run down, for, what with the sight of my bicycle, and the lashings they received from their drivers, the horses became sometimes frantic. It mattered little what I said, what I did. If I asked imperatively, or if I asked politely, for right of way, it was all the same to these Galician hogs, who, seeing I was the weakest party, would fain run me to the wall.

In the afternoon of that day out of Dukla I had carefully descended a long, winding hill. At the bottom was a small wooden bridge spanning a stream. Coming down the hill opposite were a couple of waggons, and, from where I was, I could see we should reach the bridge together. Anxious to avoid this I increased my pace, bumped over the bridge, and, keeping on the extreme edge of the roadway, endeavoured to pass the waggons.

As was usual, the horses were plunging

F

violently. The driver of the first waggon was standing up, cracking his whip, and endeavouring to keep his unruly steeds in check. As I passed him, he leaned over and, with a swift, sudden movement, made a desperate cut at me with his whip. His aim fell short, and the thong came down with a sounding thwack on the back part of the machine where was my luggage. I steered off to the left, and saw ahead the driver of the second waggon with his whip circling around his head, prepared to do for me what his companion had failed in.

Two means out of the difficulty instantly presented themselves. One was to dismount, and the second to draw my revolver. I had no occasion, however, to do either. There was another means at hand which I had not reckoned on. The horses, rearing and crying, became unmanageable, and I, having practically no roadway, went straight for them. Maddened, they turned, and, tearing the reins from the driver's hands, bolted for the side of the road. The inside wheels caught the frail posts of the bridge, which gave way like a rail of match sticks ; the wheels slipped over the side, and then horses, driver, and cart fell into the stream.

I heard shouts behind me, but I was pressing hard at the pedals. I reached the brow of the short hill and glanced back, to see the driver of the first waggon running to the assistance of his comrade ; and in the stream I saw the overturned cart with the horses lashing about in the water, and their discomfited driver up to his waist in mud, wading towards the bank. Then the bend of the road hid the scene from me, and I bumped, bumped, bumped steadily on.

Later on the road became more level, and the surface better. Well into the afternoon I came upon the outskirts of Premysal, and, refusing the reiterated offers of persistent Hebrews to show me the way to the best hotel, presently came out into a broad street, where big houses, restaurants, and *cafés* spoke of civilisation. I found an hotel which was comfortable, and did justice to my first Polish dinner, for I was now in Poland.

I have now to recount an adventure which, while not at all startling or desperate, is of so

peculiar a nature as to throw some light upon
the manners and customs of the Poles. Some
three years ago I passed through Russian Poland
on my way to Moscow, and put up at a small
inn in the town of Kalrushyn, and retired to bed.
Early in the morning I was awakened by someone
trying to open the door from the outside, and
when this was effected I saw the face of the
proprietor of the inn. What was more natural
than that I should think that, in entering my
bedroom in such a manner, he intended to rob
me? I presented my revolver, and scared him
off. Critics whose travelling experiences probably
extend to a thirty-five shilling trip to Paris at
once set this adventure down as a fabrication,
written, in fact, for the sensation-monger. But
history repeats itself, and here in Premysal, in
the Hotel National, an adventure similar in all
details, with the exception of the revolver incident, occurred.

I had retired to bed, and was sleeping soundly,
for I was tired. But I woke suddenly, and with
a start, as if something was about to happen.
Imagine my consternation to see a man in my

TYPES OF GALICIAN PEASANTS

room. Further, when that man had my jacket in his hands, and was systematically rifling the pockets.

I lay still and watched him. He removed all my papers, pocket-book, map, handkerchief, and odds and ends, which the pocket contained. His back was towards me, and he did not see that I was scrutinising his every movement. He took my waistcoat, in the watch-pocket of which I had some twenty pounds in loose gold. He took the money out and laid it on the table. He emptied the other pockets, and then took my knicker-bockers, extracted the loose coin from them, and laid that on the table. Then, gathering up my clothing, he made a move for the door.

But I was there before him; gave a grab at his shoulder, which completely swung him round. He stared at me terrified, for the expression I must have assumed was ferocious.

"Now," said I, "what's your game?"

"Please?"

"What are you doing here?"

"Your clothes!"

"Yes, my clothes; what are you doing with them?"

"I am the Boots; I am going to brush your clothes."

"Who told you to take my things from the pockets?"

"It is usual, sir; we always do it."

I rang the bell violently, and presently the head waiter appeared. He listened patiently to my somewhat hot interrogation as to the why and the wherefore of this strange proceeding. Then he smiled; then he laughed; then he burst into a loud guffaw, and said—

"Dear sir, the poor fellow is only doing his duty and a kindness for you. In Poland you should take everything out of your pockets, and put your clothes out to be brushed. That is the custom everywhere, and the Boots coming here for your clothes, kindly did for you what you neglected to do."

And when I came to Lemberg three days later, I received ample corroboration from the friends I made there. My adventure caused them amusement, but it was brought keenly home to me that when one is in Rome one must do as the Romans do, and when in Poland the visitor must empty his own pockets.

CHAPTER IX.

ACROSS THE RUSSIAN FRONTIER

I WAS riding slowly along in the direction of Lemberg, my eyes on the ground, for loose boulders and deep ruts abounded. On either side of the road ran a deep ditch half full of stagnant water, and a chance side-slip on that greasy highway might have caused an unrelishable ducking.

Five hours of this torture of a road had I had, and I was beginning to think that about enough. Lemberg seemed ever so far away, and yet it was only twenty kilometres—but think of the road!

A shout caused me to look up, and cut short the five-thousandth curse which I had levelled at Galician roads, and there, lurching painfully towards me, came a troop of cyclists some twenty strong. Men of Lemberg they were, headed by their president, Count Drobojowski, and they had come out to pilot me over the last stretch of road leading to their capital.

Now the road seemed easier, though really it was not, but when one has company, and such good company as these Lemberg cyclists, a few side-slips, or a few hard knocks from stray stones as big as flower-pots are reckoned nothing.

Once three of us subsided gracefully into the ditch; once, when endeavouring to avoid an exceedingly lively horse, the whole cavalcade fell and floundered in undignified confusion; once a machine broke down, and all hands were called to the repair; but these Polish cyclers, inured to such fearful roads, took everything in good part, and laughed when things looked least worth laughing at.   So Lemberg was reached.

Here, on the extreme edge of Austrian Poland, less than ninety miles from the Russian frontier, cycling flourishes gamely.   Lemberg, though but a small city, possesses over a thousand wheelmen, boasts a cycle track, has four clubs, and includes among the brethren of the wheel the leaders of the community.

And the city is fair.   A semi-Oriental town standing in a valley with the shadows of the blue Carpathians away in the distance.   To the east the undulating land rolls away to where a purple ridge of forest marks the commencement of the land of the Czar, and beyond that ridge lies the vast plain of Central Russia.

The day and a half I spent in Lemberg were pleasant enough, though I had much to do preparing for my lonely journey across that plain I have spoken of, for Moscow was to be the goal of my next spin, a three weeks' journey at the very least. A company of Lemberg cyclists were to accompany me to the very gates of Russia, to see me safe, they said, out of Austria.

We started one fine morning, reached the Jewish town of Brody that night, and next morning pulled out for the frontier, now only four miles away. Once again those familiar black and white posts of the Russian Emperor gleamed before me. Once again I saw the sheen of the sun on the bayonet of a Russian sentry; once again I saw that heavy bar drawn across the roadway, which seemed to say, if wood could speak, "Stop! What want you here in the land of the great white Czar?"

At the little wooden shanty of the Austrian

customs I collected the money which I had paid
as duty on my bicycle when entering the country,
shook hands with the customs officer, who good-
naturedly wished me the best of luck on my
journey, and then walked over to the bars. The
Austrian soldier on duty raised the black and
yellow bar of his country, and I passed beneath.
Three paces further the black and white barrier
of the Russian stopped me. The sentry came
forward. He was sullen, morose. " Pashport ! "
he almost growled. " Pashport ! "

I handed over the document without a word.
The sentry beckoned a comrade, and together
this precious illiterate pair mauled my passport
with their filthy fingers, the while they tried to
decipher it. Then appeared a small, bloated
individual in a white jacket, top boots, and big
peaked cap. He came up to the barrier, looked
carefully for a full minute at me, then at the
machine, and then addressed a question to me
which will for ever remain a mystery.

He took a cigarette case from his pocket,
extracted a cigarette, carefully tapped it on
the leg of his boot, and proceeded to light it.

He took two or three whiffs, rolled his eyes, and emitted the smoke from his nostrils. I gazed at him curiously, amusedly, for I knew he was only doing this for effect, just to show us poor miserable outsiders what an important thing it was to be a servant of the Czar.

He took the passport from the sentry, leaned against the gate, and proceeded to read it. Well might he have tried to read Afghan, or Chinese, as English; to him either would have been as intelligible. And yet he read carefully, slowly, smoking the while. Then he folded up my passport and stalked majestically away. There was a burst of laughter from the Lemberg cyclists, who were hanging on the Austrian barrier. The officer heard it, looked back, and scowled. One of my companions shouted "Bravo!" in ironical applause at the achievement of the Russian.

For a quarter of an hour I chatted easily with the cyclists, being all this while, mind you, in a sort of cage, between the barriers of Austria and Russia. At the end of that time the white-coated individual reappeared, stalked over to the barrier, and uttered the single word "Sudar!" ("Come here").

A hurried handshake with those good-hearted fellows who had accompanied me, and then, with much creaking, the Russian barrier was raised, and for the fourth time in my existence I set foot on Russian soil. I followed the officer into the wooden building where he had his office. As we entered he pointed at a large oleograph of the Czar on the wall; I understood him, and doffed my hat immediately.

" Have you any papers ? "

" A few—correspondence and a few newspapers."

" Oh ! Where are you going ? "

" Moscow."

" What for ? "

" Pleasure."

He pondered for a minute, then a bright idea seemed to strike him.

" Have you any business ? "

"Yes; I am a correspondent."

" Where is your Russian passport ? "

" Not necessary. I am an Englishman, and have an English passport."

" But I can't read it. How do I know it is a passport ? "

This completely floored me, and I could not answer.

"I cannot deal with you here with such a passport as this. You must go to the first town and see the police-master and the head customs officer. Give me your papers."

I handed over my pocket-book, containing my money, notes, and letters. I took my bag from the bicycle and gave him that also. These he made up into a parcel, which he sealed in about a dozen places. I was prepared for the worst!

" How far is this town ? "

" Radsilevo, five versts."

" I can ride the bicycle ? "

" No, you must walk ; a soldier will go with you."

All this conversation was the result of much labour, as I could not understand everything he said. I believe he knew the German language, but would not speak it. It was now nearly midday, and I was feeling hungry. My inquiry as to where I could get something to eat was met with the reply, " Radsilevo."

So I tramped across the fields in company with a sullen soldier, who carried my bundle and watched my every movement like a cat, as if I wanted to bolt. The sun was now high in the heavens, and I was thirsty and hungry. That five versts took us an hour and a half, for the way was deep in sand and mire. At length the little green and white church of the town appeared, and we went splashing through the mud of its only street.

"Can't we stop and have something to eat?" I said, but the soldier only shook his head.

First of all we went to the customs-house, where five intelligent officers probed the contents of my bundle. The dirty pocket-handkerchiefs, the well-worn stockings, the none-too-clean underclothing it contained puzzled them not at all, but the case of medicines absorbed their curiosity; they smelt all the drugs in turn, passed comparisons, and offered opinions.

They held a council of war as to whether they should confiscate my maps or not, as they were the Russian military survey. The argument waxed long, and meant the consumption of much time and many cigarettes. I was cross-questioned, was—but there, why go into more details of this infernal frontier business? To cross the Russian frontier by rail is as easy as crossing from Holland to Germany. To cross the Russian frontier by road is to be subjected to indignities which make your blood boil. You are the sport of every jack-in-office, who, bursting with his miserable authority, gives himself airs which the Czar himself would blush at.

At three o'clock in the afternoon the customs formalities were over. I had paid duty on my bicycle, and they let me go. But not so fast! I had yet to see the police-master, and learn what he had to say regarding my passport — which document the soldier, who still bore me guard, carried in his leather pouch.

As luck would have it, the police-master was not at home. Where was he? The unkempt gentleman in the faded uniform who answered our inquiries didn't know, and apparently didn't care. We wandered out into the roadway again, the soldier and I, and gazed meditatively at each other.

Not only was I hungry, but I was desperate. I felt in a murderous mood, and would gladly have had a hand in the death of that soldier if such had been within the regions of possibility.

I did the next wisest thing, and one which never fails in Russia. I took out my pocket-book and extracted a three-rouble note.

"Look here," said I, "I don't believe it is necessary to get that passport vizéd at all, do you?"

I toyed with the three-rouble note, and the grey eye of the soldier was glued upon it wolfishly.

"It's no use waiting here until the policemaster returns. He might not return at all to-day," said I, waving the three-rouble note. "Then what shall we do?"

"I don't think it's at all necessary," said the man, with the look of one who had all along been doing his best to befriend me

He opened his pouch and produced my passport. I dropped the three-rouble note in his pouch. He dropped the passport into my hand. I winked. He laughed. And then I hopped into the saddle and made off.

I raided the first shop I came to, bought a box of sardines, two or three cakes of chocolate, and bread. At a small *traktir* or tea-house hard by I got some tea made, and ate my none too delicate repast as only a hungry man can.

CHAPTER X.

IN LITTLE RUSSIA

WHY they call it Little Russia I don't know. It seems a very big Russia to me, counting as it does several provinces at the south-west end of the empire, and embracing a tract of land in which you might lose England, Ireland, Scotland, and Wales, and only find them after a long search.

But the inhabitants like being called Little Russians—just to distinguish themselves, it would seem, from the cold northerners; the swarthy Don Cossacks down by the Black Sea littoral; the Tartars of the centre; and those strange animals they have never seen who live beyond the far Urals, and are "Siberiaks."

In the empire itself the Little Russians are chiefly celebrated for their singing and dancing. They are the musical portion of the community.

No other Russian can dance and sing so well as this inhabitant of the south-west provinces. He is an adept at playing the accordion, can pipe in his shrill treble not unharmoniously, and when it comes to doing the Russian big boot dance he has no rival all over the world.

From the frontier to Dubno, the first town of any importance in Little Russia, was a matter of sixty versts, or forty miles, but sixty versts of land over which there is no made road. When I set out from Radsilevo it was to plough through sand several inches deep, and over a track distinguished from the common country only by the wheel marks made by many carts. Yes, there was no mistaking that this was Russia! Right and left a wilderness of sand, morass, stunted trees, willows, fir, pine, beech; a broken-down log hut here and there, nothing to speak of man's civilising hand; all suggestive of barbaric times.

Two miles from Radsilevo found me walking with my machine on my shoulder, and sand up to the calf of my leg; a drizzling rain falling, and a blustering wind soughing through the melancholy-looking trees. "How much more of it?" thought I as I stumbled and fell for the twentieth time. "How much more of it?" as I rose and shook the powdery sand out of my shoes, and wiped it out of my eyes. Up on the ridge of a hill I saw the rolling country ahead, but not a sign of life, not a human habitation.

For hours I plunged along, riding where a bare stretch of grass land would permit my wheels to revolve, and walking when sump and sand made the wheels sink inches deep into the earth. The drizzle ceased, but the black clouds glowered down upon me, and then I came upon a bifurcation in the road, and, as good luck would have it, a wandering moujik in the near distance.

"To the right," said the moujik, who looked steadfastly at my machine, "Dubno, twenty versts." He was a shock-headed individual in a red shirt, tattered velvet pantaloons, and top boots. He watched me as I lumbered off to the right, saw me fall three times, with never a smile on his face. Had he ever seen a bicycle before? It is doubtful; for when, ten minutes later, I looked back, I saw him still standing there, looking steadily after me.

It was with extreme thankfulness that late in the afternoon I espied ahead the green and white façade of Dubno's church. The sand track turned abruptly to the left, and presently I saw stretching away ahead, the great white *chaussée* of Central Russia.

What a pleasure it was then to feel the pedals flying around beneath me, to have a broad, hard road, dead level, and as fine a one as we have in England. Extremes meet in Russia. Either the best of roads or none at all. Half an hour back it was impossible to ride, now the difficulty was to keep the machine in. Dubno was reached —a small, squalid town, the main street of which was ankle deep in stinking garbage, where dilapidated houses seemed to vie with each other as to which should be the first to fall, and where my old friend the Polish Jew bobbed up serenely.

My costume betrayed the fact that I was a traveller and a stranger, therefore legitimate prey for every Jew in Dubno. It mattered little that I was firm in my announcements that I had ability enough to find for myself an hotel. Half a dozen black-bearded, evil-smelling Hebrews, the fire of avarice in their eyes, earnestly plucked my sleeves, imploring, beseeching me to come this way or that. I tramped steadily along through the filth, my escort swelling visibly as I proceeded. I saw an hotel, a mere hut though it was, and stopped. The escort stopped too. In one voice they denounced the hotel I had selected. Each one had a different hotel, all better, all cheaper. I would have none of them, however, so I picked up my bicycle and scrambled up the rickety stairs with the mob at my heels.

Seeing that I was determined to stop in the hotel I had selected, my friends the Jews had to fall back on other tactics. They quarrelled amongst themselves as to who had brought me here; all wanted tipping; all expected it, and meanwhile I had selected my room. I had comfortably housed my bicycle by my bed, and when my Jewish friends attempted to crowd in my room I slammed the door in their faces and left them to curse and spit outside.

The wind was blowing dead on the handle-bar when I pulled out from Dubno next morning. I wanted to cover at least sixty miles that day, and reach, if possible, the town of Rovno. It was, however, terrible work pushing against the blast, which came in one uninterrupted gale over a country absolutely flat and sterile. The road was level and straight and so it would go to Kieff, the great city of Southern Russia, four hundred miles further on. As I pedalled slowly along, lumbering telegas carrying land produce to distant parts would be overtaken. Their horses would shy at the strange sight of a bicycle. Drivers, invariably asleep on the tops of their loads, would awake, grab their reins, and swear heartily. Once a frightened horse plunged down a steep embankment; over went the telega, off came the driver with a sounding squelch on the grass, then boxes, bales, and other baggage hurtled and rolled down the ditch, while the last glimpse I had of the catastrophe was the horse on its back pawing the air vigorously.

About midday I stopped at a small post-station, where I was able to get some milk and bread, and it was while here that the post tarantass carrying the mails came along. It was going to Rovno, and when the horses had been changed,

and the tarantass started on its eastward journey,
I pedalled up behind it, and obtained a welcome
shelter from the gale. The twenty versts to the
next station were rattled off under the hour, and
I was beginning to congratulate myself that I
should have splendid pacing all the way to Rovno.

But I reckoned without my host. For some
reason or other the two post officials resented
my hanging on to their tarantass. Whether they
thought I wanted to rob the mails or what I
know not, but several times they waved me off.
Both these sour-looking individuals were armed
to the teeth with revolvers and swords, and once
one of them plucked forth his revolver and took
pot-shots at the telegraph posts as they flashed
by. "Could it be," thought I, "that this individual imagined he would scare me off by an
arrogant display of his weapons?" So I glued on
all the tighter. Once the road narrowed to cross
a bridge, and here we overtook a long caravan.
The yemshik of the tarantass howled and cracked
his whip, while he urged his horses to their top-
most pace. We cleared the bridge almost at a
bound, but the tarantass slowed a bit, and I was

forced to run up alongside. I instantly put on the brake, but then the yemshik did a dastardly trick. He pulled his horses right over and crowded me into the ditch. My pedal struck one of the rear wheels of the vehicle, and instantly I fell with a crash.

I was up again in a moment, unhurt, save for a few scratches, and saw the tarantass careering along with those two amiable subjects of his Majesty Nicholas II. hanging over the back convulsed with laughter at my mishap. Then over the brow of the short hill they disappeared, and I was left to rub my bruises and gaze with sorrowful eyes upon a badly bent pedal.

Late that same afternoon I reached Rovno, after I had, with the aid of some stones, straightened my pedal spindle. All my old hate of Russia was beginning to come back to me, for it seemed impossible in this country to meet one man who had a spark of human feeling for a stranger. There was the same disturbance in Rovno as in Dubno; but I was in a truculent mood, and not disposed to either politeness or even common good manners. I locked my bicycle up in my room, and then went out and prowled in the street to find a shop whereat to buy some food.

I got some sardines, a loaf of bread, and half a pound of sausage, and as I was bearing these comestibles in triumph to my room, a carriage drawn by a pair of spirited horses came briskly along the roadway. The occupant of the carriage, a young and decidedly un-Russian looking individual, stared hard at me as I passed. I was at the door of my hotel when I heard the carriage coming back. The young man descended hurriedly, came straight up to me, raised his hat, and said in most excellent English—

"Excuse me, sir, but are you not an Englishman?"

I nearly dropped my sardines, sausage, and bread, as I burst out with—

"Yes; why, certainly!"

"Well, we've got a telegraph station of the Overland Indo-European Telegraph Company here. I thought you were an Englishman when I first saw you, and it struck me that you might like to come up to the office and look over some English papers."

I looked hard at him.

"Surely," I cried, "you are Mr. Walters, whom I met in Warsaw three years ago!"

He fell back a pace or two.

"Well, I'm——" Then he stopped; he seemed at a loss for words, but the saving sentence of every Englishman came to his aid.

"Come and have a drink," said he.

CHAPTER XI.

A NIGHT WITH THE MOUJIKS

I HAD left Kieff, the capital of Little Russia, and was ploughing my way northwards towards the great Central Russian *chaussée* which leads to Moscow. Ploughing, I say, and it was ploughing, for the full force of a north-easterly blast bore upon my front wheel. Grey skies were overhead, skies of scurrying clouds; not a glimpse of the blue, and not for seven days had I seen the sun.

Right and left of me the dull, uninteresting swamp country stretched; vistas of morass and sandy dunes; clumps of willows, with long leaves stretched out before the wind; long lush grass tossing and sighing; lakelets and slimy bog-water, ruffled and angry with the gale.

A wind to make one strain at the pedals and lurch and strain again; a wind which sang through the spokes; a wind which roared in one incessant roar in the ears; a wind which brought the dry alkali-like dust from the sand dunes and smothered one.

For six days had I laboured like this, but at length I rolled into Chernigoff, a decent enough town, where I found an inn of more than average Russian cleanliness, and realised that from here I had a full thousand versts to cover before I caught a sight of Moscow's Kremlin.

Hardly had I got into mine inn, before, as a matter of fact, I had finished negotiating with its shock-headed proprietor on the possibilities of tea, eggs, and bread, large raindrops fell, and five minutes later thunder was booming, hail was rattling, and lightning quivering in the dense atmosphere. All evening and all night it rained like a deluge. I ventured out once and splashed about in the mud of the roadway in a devil-may-care spirit, but somehow I was thankful, for I hoped the rain might mean a change of wind.

The sun shone intermittently when I left Chernigoff, and as I bumped slowly over the stones and then over the long wooden bridge, rain - soaked moujiks, with their caravans of telegas, were toiling into town. Sorry they looked, with horses caked to the shoulders in mire, and vehicles mere moving masses of mud. I cast one last look at Chernigoff's green and white church as I slowly turned the corner, and then the rolling country was spread before me.

Had the wind dropped? Scarcely a bit, and as mile after mile I struggled along over this bleak country, it seemed rather to increase. Midday came and passed. In a lone hut by the wayside I had partaken of a humble meal of black bread and tea—all the poor moujik had to give me; and now, miles and miles from human habitation, I was lurching along, and it was raining miserably.

Mackintoshes! As useless as paper in such tropical rains as those of Southern Russia. I was soaked to the skin ere an hour had elapsed. From every part of the machine streams of water descended. Off the road-bed the rain ran in torrents to the ditches, themselves overflowing and lapping into the fields beyond.

Think of it, ye English wheelmen in our own fair

country, where, when rain does fall, always have you the prospect of that comfortable inn where dry clothes, where succulent food and kindly welcome await you ; but here no hope of shelter at all, unless, like magic, some moujik's hut should sprout into being, and where, though the hut may be like a sieve, one can get the glimpse of a human face.

Late in the afternoon I saw a post-station. A wooden building, standing in a perfect lake. I made for it at once, and pushed into the doorway, leaving a trail of water behind me like a river. There was not a soul in the place, and I sat down on a bench, exhausted, desperate. I was hungry, tired, drenched to the skin, and here was a Government post-station, the only hope of refuge for the traveller, and deserted.

For an hour I waited, looking through the broken window at the pitilessly descending rain, and then, from afar off, I heard the monotonous jangle of bells, followed by the bellowing voice of a man roaring out an indescribable Russian song.

A tarantass heaved in sight, and through the mist of rain I saw an individual in the vehicle

THE MOUJIK AT SAMOVAR

THE DANCE, A LA RUSSE

prone on his back, his legs over the side, while he waved a vodki bottle in his hand. The yemshik on the front seat seemed asleep, or drowned, for the water fell off every corner of him ; but he was simply drunk, as was his master, his Majesty's servant, post-horse superintendent of the station.

The horses stopped, the yemshik rolled off his perch into the mud, the postmaster slowly uncurled himself from the bottom of the tarantass, lurched over the side, and scrambled on all fours up the steps of the house. He reeled into the room where I was, saw me, stopped, gasped, and blinked. Then he said something, and punctuated what he said with waves of the vodki bottle.

My appearance had sobered him a little, for he thought at first I was a chinovnik and wanted horses. But then he saw my bicycle, and then he saw the streams of water in the room, and he reeled towards me with "What do you want? What do you want?"

"Food and shelter," I replied.

"No food, no shelter—hic !—post-station; horses. Do you—hic !—want horses?"

" No ; only some food."

" No food ; go away."

" Give me some bread, then."

No bread ; go away."

He reeled around, made for the door, missed it, and fell headlong. He lay where he fell, an inert mass of drunken humanity. I stepped over his body and went to the door. The yemshik was on the doorstep dead drunk, and under a douche of water falling from the eaves. I was desperate.

I went to the various rooms of the station determined to steal food if I could get at it. All the rooms were locked. I returned to the main apartment, a loathing for everything Russian within me.

I seized my bicycle and wheeled it over the prostrate body of the postmaster; I jabbed the back wheel in his side as I did so—he merely grunted—got outside, mounted in the little river which was a road, and made off. No cessation in the rain, no particle of hope of getting shelter, it seemed; but when after two hours' miserable riding I saw off to the right a cluster of wooden huts I felt quite happy.

I waded through the ditch at once, and with my eye on the best-looking house of the village, splashed over a field. Out of the small two-foot-square window peeped a man's head—a shaggy head, with the hair blowing about like yellow grass. The head stared at me blankly as I approached. It disappeared as I drew even nearer; the door of the hut was opened, and without further ceremony I went in.

Imagine a small room fifteen feet by fifteen, so low that one could hardly stand upright. Rough wooden walls with hay-packing between the logs, a wooden floor through which the water was oozing. In the corner a stone stove, on the top of which were piled heaps of sheepskins—this the bed of the moujik. In another corner a sapling depended from the wall, on the end of which a small tray hung—this the cradle of the moujik's baby; a bench along one side; a roughly-made table in the centre. Such was the moujik's house.

" God be with you, little father ; but from where do you come in such weather ? "

I answered him, and he moved about to get

H

me food. A chunk of black bread, that was all he had to give. But presently a bedraggled female splashed in out of the mire; as she entered she crossed herself reverently before the small image of the Virgin in the corner. She would prepare the samovar for me, she said, if I had tea with me—which I had.

Then on that rough table, with the hissing samovar before us, we three made a meal of black bread, and tea without sugar. But somehow my arrival had become known in the village. It was whispered abroad that a *barin* had sought shelter, and moujiks came lumbering in. One contributed a couple of eggs to the feast, and another intimated that for fifty kopecs he could buy a quart of vodki.

"Vot! vot! but you are a *bolshoi chelavek* (a great man)," said they when I gave the fifty kopecs, and the vodki was brought. Chilled to the bone as I was, I drank the horrible spirit greedily. It seemed like drinking fire, and sent the blood dancing through my veins. More moujiks came in, and I bought another bottle of vodki. We all drank except the woman. The moujiks became loquacious, and my quaint Russian seemed to interest them.

The technicalities of the bicycle they were never tired of penetrating. Then the two sons of the woodman returned from their day's labour and helped to swell the crowd. Another samovar was prepared, more vodki was got. One of the sons brought out an accordion and began playing one of those wild airs beloved of the Little Russians. A big-booted moujik bounced into the middle of the room and commenced dancing.

How he clapped his heels together; how he bounced up and down; how he circled the room at lightning pace on his haunches; while the accordion squealed and droned, and the audience laughed and clapped its hands in accompaniment, meanwhile that the night had come down and the rain had ceased. Then one by one they shook my hand and called me *karoshee chelavek* —for had I not bought them vodki and supplied them with cigarettes? One by one they took their departure, howling out their songs as they splashed into the night.

The old woman made up a bed of sacks for

me on the floor, and side by side with her two big sons I laid myself down. The moujik and his wife sought repose on the stove; the baby in its swinging cradle piped its shrill treble. Rats scratched at the wooden flooring; insects crawled and crept; outside I could hear the wind sighing dismally, and the raindrops splashing from the roof. Then I slept.

CHAPTER XII.

ON THE CENTRAL RUSSIAN
CHAUSSÉE

ONE morning I lurched out of the narrow path-like road, leading from Kieff to Mogilev, into the centre of a broad, white highway, stretching right and left as far as the eye could see.

A lonely post station was stuck at this juncture of four roads, and a tall black and white post stood like a sentinel in the middle of a grassy slope. It read :—

To Warsaw	. .	$631\frac{1}{2}$ versts.
To Moscow	. .	$551\frac{1}{4}$ versts.
To Petersburg	. .	882 versts.

The spot was familiar to me. Three years previously I had twice pedalled by this very station, this very post, going to and coming from Moscow, when I had been vain enough to attempt the establishment of a bicycle record between the capital of Britain and the Kremlin city.

Now, however, my desires were more peaceful and gentle; I hung not my head over the handle-bar and rode furiously as then. There was no limit on the time I might take in getting to Khiva. There was no need for me to fret if the steady head wind caused the pace to be slow. And there was something of satisfaction in that, for the post conjured up the reminiscences of my record ride, of the anxieties which I experienced when, almost night and day, I was piling on the versts, the one thing uppermost in my mind being to do what I had said; though the world knew little about it—and cared less.

So I turned my front wheel in the direction of Moscow, 551¼ versts away. The post-station and the black and white wooden sentinel faded into the horizon behind, and before me stretched the wide, undulating plain of Central Russia. Lonely, bleak, and inhospitable it looked, scantily culti-vated, groups of stunted bushes here and there, stretches of silent, steely water, treacherous bogs or sandy dunes, these latter showing up glaringly in the white light of the Russian sun.

It is impossible to enthuse over a bicycle ride

in Russia. Think of it—a great road running as straight as a die for nearly a thousand miles, and, dotted on this, only a few squalid villages or tumble-down, forlorn-looking towns.

Excitement there is none, except that occasionally offered by a runaway horse or a group of moujiks, the latter always ready to make sport of the bicycle by hurling insults, and sometimes more substantial missiles, at the unoffending bicyclist. People talk about the enormous number of cycles in Russia, yet here had I already covered over a thousand miles of the best Russian roads, and, barring my own, had not seen a single wheel. Clear it is that the cycle is a *rara avis* on this Central Russian *chaussée*.

My appearance in a village is the signal for a wholesale gathering of the clans. Old men, young men, old women, young women, children, and dogs come tumbling out of their houses, and fall over each other in order to be first in the road to get a near glimpse of the "samokat," as the bicycle is called. Ragged-haired brutes of the canine tribe bare their gums and lick their chops in anticipation of a piece of succulent British calf, and then come with yelps and snarls to the fray. Red-shirted, tow-headed moujiks, grinning like apes, shout incomprehensible questions. Slatternly women, more or less naked, and oft with hanging busts showing indecently, scream and howl with laughter. Urchins diligently collect the foulest dung with which to pelt me. Truly, the bicycle inspires no respect amongst these moujiks.

One Sunday evening I rode steadily along through the filth of the only street in the Jewish town of Cherikov. A mild-eyed Hebrew whom I accosted asserted that there was no inn at all, but a friend of his, a clean and honest Jew, could let me have a room. As for food, well, it was pos-sible that this town of eight thousand inhabitants might with trouble rake together a few eggs, some black bread, and perhaps a bowl of milk. The honest Jew received me cordially, and gave me an apartment which, though smelling somewhat sour from years of bugs, was, at any rate, a shelter.

Like a fly into the spider's web I went. I ate my eggs and drank my milk; I wrote postcards, and then I slept. Slept! well, I worried through the night, and in the morning was only too anxious to get away. But six roubles (thirteen shillings) for three eggs, two pints of milk, and the comfort of a buggy bed, was, I thought, too extravagant a price to pay. I intimated to my host that I was merely an ordinary traveller; I was not going through the country in order to keep the entire population for years to come. I spoke gently but firmly, and wound up by intimating that I thought a rouble for the bed and a rouble for the food would yield a handsome profit if carefully calculated. More, at any rate, I didn't intend to pay.

The Jew listened calmly to my argument, all the time busily searching in the innermost recesses of his underclothing for the predatory flea. He had been accustomed, he said, to charge six roubles. He shrugged his shoulders. Six roubles he would have.

I put on my hat, slung my camera over my shoulder, and went to the room where my bicycle was. The fellow had locked the door and taken away the key. I lost my temper then, and began to expostulate. The Jew looked on undisturbed. The Jew's wife, a hawk-nosed female, smelling horribly of onions, laughed. I pulled and tugged at the door, and then I kicked it.

"Will you pay six roubles?" asked the Jew with a grin.

"Never!" said I, with another kick at the door. "Open the door, or I'll break it down."

"Shall I call the police?"

Police! I had never thought of that. In a moment I was out of the house, and commenced to wander the town in search of the police-station. I found it at length A heavily-armed individual, badly in want of a shave, accosted me. What did I want? The police-master? Well, the police-master was asleep. I must come in an hour's time. In my broken Russian I explained the situation, and my friend the policeman laughed consumedly.

I sat on the doorstep and waited for the police-master to wake. The unshaved one, at the expiration of an hour and a half, intimated that I could be received. I found the police-master with eyes gummed and blubbed by sleep, half undressed, and toying with a glass of lemon-coloured hot water called tea.

I explained how things stood. He listened moodily, like a man who had no interest in life, sipping the hot water at intervals. He laughed once, a sniggering laugh, which made my blood boil. Forthwith I produced all the documents I had on me, and their effect upon him was magical. He forgot all about his tea. He even got up to shake my hand. Why had I not come to him the previous night? he asked. Shameful that I should have had to put up with such accommodation. He busied himself with his toilet. He got into a pair of big boots; he donned a white coat with gorgeous buttons; he buckled on a heavy sword; and surmounted the whole with a wide-peaked cap, in which scintillated the cockade of the Czar.

Then we sallied forth—police-master, two dusty, tired-looking policemen, and myself. The Jew saw us coming and came out to explain his side of the case. The two policemen promptly swept him into the roadway. We entered the house with the jingling of spurs.

"Open the door!" said the police-master, producing his cigarette case and offering me a *papiros*.

"Open the door!" The trembling female with the hawk nose unlocked the door, and I pulled forth my bicycle. "What shall I give them for what I have had?" I asked the police-master.

"Nothing at all," answered that worthy.

I shook hands with the police-master, and we exchanged cards. We went out on to the door-step, and in answer to his inquiries, I related what I was doing in Russia. The two policemen listened intently; a little group of silent Jews had collected in the road.

My honest host was sitting on the kerb; the hawk-nosed female had disappeared. Then I shook hands again with the police-master. The policemen touched their caps to me. I hopped on my bicycle; the Jews scattered, and two minutes later Cherikov was away back.

Wonderful are the effects of a few pieces of official paper in Russia. Someone has written that the machinery of Russian administration is clogged by formality and ceremony. I have already learned to appreciate the value of being "papered" through the Russian Empire. With no papers one is worse off than a dog. A prince of the blood, unarmed with official documents, is at the mercy of the commonest peasant. A man is not a man in Russia. He is a paper, and the bigger that paper and the weightier it is, the heavier the seals and the larger the stamps, so he is relegated to his proper standard of importance.

A few days later I passed through Roslavl, and left behind me the last traces of original ¬Poland. I was now in the country of the true Slav. The route became hilly, but the road was ever straight ahead. Through Yuknov to Malo-Yaroslavitz, site of the great battle between Napoleon and the Russian Cossacks. I looked upon the black iron monument, erected in memory of that great event, and thought of 1812 and 1854 and the present, when everything popular in France is Russian, and everything popular in Russia is French. Podolsk was passed one bright, hot day. I came at length to the top of the Sparrow hills, where Napoleon had watched the burning of Moscow, and saw below me the great white city glittering in the afternoon sun.

CHAPTER XIII.

TOWARDS EAST RUSSIA

IT was a broiling hot day in the month of June when a little party of cyclists assembled by arrangement at the octroi post on the Nigni-Novgorod high road, five versts outside Moscow city. First there was Georges Zemlicska, one of the leading lights of cycling Russia; then Elia Wassilovitch Orloff, one of the founders of the cycling industry in Moscow; then Ivan Ivanovitch Golamsine, editor of Russia's principal cycling paper; then Otto Hubner, whose name is sufficiently German for all purposes of identification; then Fred Del Strother, a Russianised Englishman; then a dozen or more wheelmen and friends; and then myself, a Rover bicycle, a camel-hair suit, top boots, and a cork helmet.

The programme for the first day out was not ambitious, a distance of sixty versts to the small

town of Bogorodsk, and no less than two cyclists
had volunteered to bear me company for at least
ten versts. Candidly, I wished they had let me go
alone, for in that ten versts both fell three times,
and one of them, lurching right across my front
wheel, caused me to execute a manœuvre which,
for dexterity, certainly equalled the best of a trick
rider's feats. Therefore I was not sorry when we
parted, and I shaped my course, once more alone,
towards the East.

When, two years previously, I had travelled
over this same road to Nigni-Novgorod, the surface had been by no means bad; but now it was
abominable. The winter had been severe, and
the road, a made *chaussée*, had been broken to
its very foundation. Two huge ruts ran down
the centre; great boulders and loose stones
bestrewed the sides; deep sand, and deeper grass
and bramble occurred at intervals.

Sometimes the road narrowed in until it was
no wider than a footpath, and such a footpath,
knee deep in long, dry grass. Dead trees, white
and withered, lay like forest corpses here and
there. Sometimes a shallow stream pursued its

way across the road, and once a bridge had stood here, the only evidence remaining being a few black and rotting timbers hanging sullenly over the water.

Pushing, carrying, sometimes riding the bicycle, I pursued my way. Through tumble-down, melancholy villages; past lone wooden huts, or some wayside tea-house, where a few frouzy and vodki-besotten moujiks held revel. Fierce and without pity the sun sent down its long shafts of heat, until one gasped as the hot air scarce seemed to satisfy inhalation, and the perspiration poured in steady streams from off one's face.

Hard work it was in goodly truth, and none could have been more gratified than I when this lonely and laborious day came to an end, and the huddle of houses in the distance announced the proximity of Bogorodsk. Here was rest at any rate, though the fare was poor, and my bed a ragged mattress as odorous as it was odious, and my room the camping-ground of thousands of black and vicious-tongued flies. I felt it more, perhaps, since but a few hours back I had been in what was at least a civilised city.

A RELIGIOUS PROCESSION IN CENTRAL RUSSIA

I wheeled out next day towards Pokroff and
Vladimir, intent upon doing a distance of 120
versts. The day promised fair, but a stiff wind
was blowing in my teeth, and the work over such
roads was hard. Now the way became hilly, not
hilly such as we know hills in England, but hilly
because of the villainous surface.

Midday found me in Pokroff, where I fell into
goodly hands, for a couple of lieutenants of the
First Little Russian Regiment were stationed
here, and were on the look out for me. Instead
of the shelter, therefore, of a Russian hostinitca,
which I already knew well enough to know as
being bad, I ate a dinner which would have done
credit to Moscow itself. The officers having travelled, and, moreover, being educated in more
languages than Russian, were as completely
different from the ordinary chinovnik as it was
possible to conceive.

Would I stop in Pokroff for just this one night?
They begged that I would stay, but the stern
realisation of the enormous distance which yet lay
before me compelled me to decline the proffered
hospitality. So once more I set out eastward.

I

The copper sun declined in the heavens. My shadow, which now lay straight out, lengthened considerably; in an hour it was a giant; in two it stretched, it seemed, to the very horizon. Blood-red old Sol went down, and the primrose rays stretching along the western hills tipped with glory those barren eminences. Then was the time to see this gaunt land of Russia robbed of some of its sterility, for, with the softening twilight, the mists and the shadows, and the quivering sun rays, nature suggested better things.

And I bumped on, jerking laboriously at the pedals, crashing and smashing through the loose stones, the sand, and the sun-baked clay. For hours I kept on, and never a soul did I see. Of life itself only some scuttling mole, some vagrant hare, some melancholy stork, some bird of gorgeous plumage, and once a long black snake lying lengthways on the roadway, which reared its ugly head and sent out its forked tongue as I rattled by.

Then it was dark, and the scope of one's vision narrowed in. I could not see the stones now, and had to ride carefully. Ahead the way was absolutely black; behind, when I looked, only a faint lemon-coloured streak along the hilltops betokening the passage of the sun on its westward journey—and Vladimir was still twenty-five miles away. Now and again, when my front wheel struck some more than usually large stone, I floundered off; now and again I would flop into a rut, and bang! bang! bang! would go the pedals on either side until, with a lurch, I was sent sprawling. Once I came to a long downhill stretch; the bottom I could not see, for it was enveloped in blackness. I kept a nervous hand on the brake lever, and pressed back the pedals.

Then, with a suddenness that was truly awful, a great black gap yawned at my very feet. I realised what it was; a gorge, the bridge across which had fallen in. I flung myself from the saddle in the nick of time, and fell, machine and all, on the very brink of a precipice. Some few stones rattled down into the depths below—how deep I know not, for it was black to sinister, and looked like the jaws of the infernal regions.

For some moments I lay there bathed in the cold perspiration brought forth by the reaction of my narrow escape. I felt faint to sickness, and so weak that when I arose and lifted up my bicycle I felt that I could not go on. But go on I must. I searched around carefully and found off to the right a narrow zigzag pathway, which led down to the bottom of the gorge and up the other side. By this means I crossed, walked up the long hill to the top, remounted, and crept cautiously over the plateau which was stretched before me.

A lonesome and fearsome ride, for I knew not at what moment some new danger would present itself. At last, away ahead, I saw a spark of light blinking solemnly in the all-pervading darkness. My heart beat with thankfulness, for this heralded a village, surely. Worse and worse became the road, and I was forced to walk. As I neared the village a monotonous "click-clack! click-clack! click-clack!" came to my ears.

It was the watchman of the village going his round and beating his wooden clapper in order to frighten thieves away, or warn them of his coming. I saw then that the light I had perceived was not stationary, but bobbed about in will-o'-the-wisp fashion, and as I got nearer I became aware that it was carried by the watchman himself.

Soon to the right and the left the ghostly outlines of low wooden houses showed themselves, but not a sign of life anywhere. I directed my footsteps towards the light, which seemed to be somewhere in the middle of the road, but stationary now, the "click-clack! click-clack!" of the watchman's rattle sounding weirdly on the night air and blending in strange concert with the croaking of hundreds of frogs in the ditches and the "chirp! chirp! chirp!" of crickets.

Then into the glare of the watchman's lantern I went. I opened my mouth to speak, but the "click-clack! click-clack! click-clack!" ceased even as a stentorian yell pierced the air. Down with a crash fell the lantern, and then I heard the sound of scurrying footsteps.

The watchman had fled! Fled, and left me his extinguished lantern as a souvenir. Poor fellow! I cannot wonder at his terror, for it is probable he had seldom or never seen a bicycle, least of all in the middle of the night. Under other circumstances I should have laughed, but as it was I was tired, hungry, and nerve-shattered.

I only cursed.

I got off the road and went to the first house and knocked long and patiently, but without avail. One after another I tried the houses, until, losing patience, I kicked and banged at one door, determined to be heard. In a few minutes I heard the sound of footsteps, the small window of the hut was opened, and the shock head of a moujik was thrust into the night.

"Shelter, if you please," I cried.

The eyes in the shock head looked at me askance.

"Shelter, if you please," I repeated, but the shock head seemed to be dumb. At length the half-expected "Neot! neot!" ("No! no!") greeted my ears.

"Open the door!"

"Neot! neot!"

"Give me a drink, then; some milk, perhaps."

"Neot! neot!"

The window was banged to, and I was left to

my own devices. There was nothing for it, so
I gathered up my bicycle and trundled off to
the road. I hopped on, set foot to pedal, and
left the village behind me. Two hours later,
famished and surly, I was banging at the door
of an hotel in Vladimir.

I was brilliantly impolite to the ragged, head-
scratching porter who opened the door. I got in,
and I was in such a mood that I think it would
have taken more than the porter to have put me
out again.

CHAPTER XIV.

NIGNI-NOVGOROD THE FAMOUS

I HAD passport difficulties in Vladimir. I was dozing comfortably in the morning when a heavy-booted policeman tramped into my room and shook me roughly by the shoulder. The tow-headed youth, who performed the duties of chambermaid, stood behind the policeman as if he was there to back him up in whatever nefarious designs the representative of law and order had upon me. My passport, it appeared, was all out of order. I had given it to the porter the night previous, and my presence was now desired at the police-station in order that I might explain myself.

I had already, in four years' experience of Russia, learned sufficient to realise the impossibility of arguing the matter out with a policeman. There was nothing for me but to obey. I would

SUNDAY IN CENTRAL RUSSIA

EAST RUSSIAN ARCHITECTURE

gladly have had another hour or two's rest, but
that was not to be thought of. I rose with a sigh,
made my toilet, and then we tramped out into
the hot streets, the policeman taking the lead,
and the tow-headed boy bringing up the rear.

The police-master was the surliest individual
I had ever met. He smoked *papiros* at a furious
rate; he drank unlimited quantities of lemon-
coloured tea; he spat and gurgled, and made all
sorts of horrible noises; he growled and hic-
coughed over my passport, demanding to know
why it was that I had not presented myself at the
police-office on the previous evening.

The explanation that I had not arrived in
Vladimir until the small hours availed little, and
it was apparent to me that there was something
wrong, for I noticed pinned to my passport were
several official-looking documents bearing huge
seals.

Finding that we could not get on very well
together in the Russian language, the police-
master gave the constable peremptory orders to
take me to another room. I was at first amused
at the arbitrary manner in which I was being

treated, but when it came to having to sit in a small, filthy room, where somnolent policemen lay stretched on benches snoring with great gusto, I became somewhat angry. "What was the matter with my passport?" I demanded of the policeman. But the policeman simply answered, "I do not speak your language. Don't talk. I cannot understand you." Half an hour passed, and I was summoned again to the presence of the police-master. "You cannot have your passport," he said, "until I have communicated with Moscow. Is it true that you took photographs of the soldiers in Pokroff?"

For a moment I was silent, and then gradually the realisation of the position I was in began to steal over me. I remembered that while in Pokroff I had seen some soldiers drilling on a plain adjacent, and had secured permission from the two officers whose acquaintance I had made, to use my kodak upon them. I well knew the suspicion attached to a man carrying a camera, especially when the camera was used by a stranger upon anything connected with the country's fortifications or military affairs. What was to be done? I explained to the police-master that it was true I had photographed some soldiers, but that I had received permission to do so. Then I fell back upon what had always saved me in my diplomatic relations with Russian officials. I pulled out my big bundle of papers and spread them before him, but was chagrined to find that he refused to look at them.

"Excuse me, your excellency," I said as politely as I could, "these papers will explain everything if you will only read them."

"They are nothing to do with me," he said loftily; "I do not want to read them. I only know that you took photographs of the soldiers at Pokroff, and that I cannot let you leave Vladimir until I have heard from Moscow. You may go, and call again to-morrow morning."

There was no help for it. I folded up my papers and wandered out into the street. When a Russian official makes up his mind to be nasty, the best thing to do is to humour him and let him enjoy the full spell of his brief authority. I went out into the street, and walked down the hill to where a white and green church marked the end of the town. I sat down on the kerb to think matters out, and the more I thought of them the more angry I became. I was on the point of walking back, intent upon telegraphing to Moscow, when a burly individual on a bicycle came wobbling over the stones. The sight was an inspiration. I went out into the road, doffed my hat, and spoke to the cyclist. He listened to me, and then burst into a guffaw of laughter.

"Speak in German, Mr. Jefferson," he said; "you speak it better than you do Russian, bad as your German is. You seem to have forgotten me altogether. Don't you remember meeting me in Nigni-Novgorod two years ago? Why, man, I have been waiting here two days for you! Pollock, in Nigni, telegraphed me that you had left Moscow, and I came across country from my works in order to see you. Now, what is all the trouble?"

I could have embraced him. I remembered him now; a big manufacturer of Portland cement near Nigni-Novgorod, an enthusiastic cyclist, and a most important man in Russia. Off we trotted to the hotel. A samovar was ordered, a bottle of brandy was put before us, and then I unfolded my predicament. How Herr Kaufmann laughed! laughed until the tears ran down his cheeks, and his sides fairly shook.

"Come with me," he said, "and we shall see some fun." He took my papers and looked at them; read them. "Splendid!" he said, "splendid! That fool of a police-master would get one of the biggest wiggings a police-master ever had if this got to the ears of the General Governor. Ivan Ivanovitch is one of my best friends; we will go round and see him."

"In this costume," I said; "surely he won't receive me?"

"If you went there without trousers," said Herr Kaufmann, "and you were a friend of mine, he would receive you. Come!"

We took a drosky to the palatial residence of the General Governor, and were bowed in to his presence before ten minutes had elapsed. White-coated and gold-epauletted individuals flitted here and there. Ivan Ivanovitch, General Governor of the province of Vladimir, shook my hand warmly and almost embraced Herr Kaufmann. They chatted in Russian for a long time, then Herr Kaufmann unfolded my little trouble. For a moment his excellency looked grave. Then his eyes began to twinkle, and the corners of his mouth to curl, and he laughed as heartily as did Kaufmann. He took out his card case, wrote something on the back of a card, and handed it to him. Tea was brought in, and after consuming a glass Herr Kaufmann and I departed, not, however, until the General Governor had made several kind inquiries concerning myself, and promised to give orders that I should not be molested or interfered with during the rest of my progress through his government.

The drosky rattled to the police office. When the policeman saw Kaufmann get out and take my arm as we walked up the stairs, he fell back with an amazed look on his face. We brushed by him and walked into the presence of the police-master.

"Well!" cried Kaufmann, "and how is his excellency the police-master?" and he sat on the table dangling his fat legs and laughing hugely.

As for the police-master, he lay back in his chair, and looked with consternation upon the German and upon myself.

"Next time," said the German, "an Englishman comes along and asks you to read his papers, be considerate a little, my friend, and read them. Now oblige me by first reading the papers of Mr. Jefferson, and secondly by reading this little card from the General Governor."

Then the police-master took my papers and read them, or at least he read the first few lines of the most important one. He grew angry with himself and snapped his fingers. He was in that sort of passion when a man feels like kicking himself. I could see the card of the General Governor made him wink. I could not read what was on it myself, but there was something evidently calculated to disturb the police-master. He muttered something about fools and interfering people, then took my passport, came round the table, and placed it in my hand; grasped my hand and shook it fervently, apologising and expostulating in the same breath. "Sit down, my dear sir, sit down. Let us have

some tea and vodki. Sit down, good Mr. Kaufmann. What a wretched mistake!"

An incident like this serves to illustrate pretty
forcibly the suspicion which is attached to any
stranger travelling through holy Russia. After
all it was but a paltry thing which had detained
me. The police-master actually had no right to
bar my progress, but, like some policemen of our
own country, he was probably spoiling for something to do. It appeared that a busybody in
Pokroff had seen me taking photographs of the
soldiers, and learning that I was an Englishman,
immediately jumped to the conclusion that I was
a spy. He telegraphed to Vladimir, and the
police-master saw a chance of distinction not to
be let slip.

Perforce it had cost me a day's delay, but I
had the satisfaction of revenge in getting my legs
under the table of the police-master that same
evening, and enjoying a capital dinner. Police-
masters, even Russian police-masters, are human.
In their official capacity they are hogs of the
most pronounced type. As host in his own
home, a more sociable, more entertaining, more

hospitable fellow surely never breathed than the police-master of Vladimir.

Next morning I pulled out for Nigni-Novgorod, which I hoped to make in three days. Herr Kaufmann would accompany me for the first day, but he regretted his inability to come with me the whole way to the Volga-side city. For the first fifty versts the road was fair enough, but then degenerated alarmingly. We stayed that night in a small village, and sheltered in the cleanest hut that we could find there. It was wonderful to see the bowing and scraping on the part of the moujiks before the great German manufacturer, Herr Kaufmann.

Next day I was alone once more, trundling heavily over the wretched roads, battling with mosquitoes, through a long stretch of swampy forest land nearing Nigi-Novgorod. I covered a good distance that day in spite of the vileness of the way, meeting not a soul on the road since I had left Vladimir. Therefore on the afternoon of the eighth day out of Moscow I was wheeling rapidly down the long slope towards the banks of the Oka. Nigni, on the opposite bank, lay

K

white and glittering. Here was bustle and excitement. The people were preparing for the great fair which was to open in a few weeks' time. Electric trams dashed hither and thither; heavily laden telegas formed great toiling caravans all along the road; the mighty Volga lay shining on my left; the sinuous Oka was before me. Over the Bridge of Boats, and I had arrived. Thomas Pollock, of Manchester and Russia, was shaking my hand and welcoming me for the second time to the city of the great fair.

Nigni-Novgorod is, perhaps, the most picturesque town in Russia north of the Caucasus. Built on a tongue of land formed by the confluence of the Oka with the Volga, its houses rise in terraces of white and green from the banks of the rivers to the top of the bluff hills which extend right along the southern shore of the Volga. Seen from the left bank of the Oka (where, by the way, is the fair-town), Nigni-Novgorod gives one the impression of an Oriental city. There is nothing sombre about it. It is a mass of colour, pretty villas nestling in groves of young trees, with here and there the brazen cupolas of the national church flashing their golden light; while, high above all, the ancient citadel, or Kremlin, frowns down upon both rivers.

And the rivers are full of life and movement; the wharves and landing stages are many and ponderous. Barges laden with wood, which have come down the Kama from the Ural mountains, are discharging their cargoes; and the Volga steamers, three-deckers on the American plan, laden with caviare for Moscow and St. Petersburg, and sometimes with passengers from the Caspian provinces, remind one of the Mississippi.

The Volga is the great water-way of European Russia, and the fleet of steamers which ply its waters would surprise those who think that Russia is a hundred years behind the times. Happening to have an introduction to one of the owners of the fleet, I had full opportunities of inspecting some of the best craft. Among these was the *Mississippi*, a prototype of all the big steamers on the American rivers, lighted with electricity, and fired with naphtha. It is fitted up like a palace, and is only one of a big fleet similarly equipped. The trade carried on by these steamers consists mainly of caviare and passengers. The finest caviare is taken from the fish of the Caspian. It is packed and loaded at Astrakhan, at the mouth of the Volga, and sent to Nigni-Novgorod, where it is distributed to the epicures of civilised Russia. The passenger traffic is enormous, two steamers leaving Nigni and Astrakhan daily, and barely sufficing for the demands.

On the low-lying west bank of the Oka, and quite apart from Nigni, is the site of the world-famous annual fair. My impression of the fair of Nigni-Novgorod is now completely different from what it was before my visit, and is far different, I daresay, to what many thousands of Englishmen picture it. A huge town, four miles wide by four and a half long, is the site of the fair. One-storey brick houses, with shops on the bazaar principle, line the streets, which are made at right angles, whilst there are boulevards and gardens, bath-houses, and a magnificent municipal building. But here the wonderment of the whole thing comes in. For ten months out of the year the magnificent fair-town has not a single inhabitant; every magazine is locked and barred, and its owner, in his Siberian or Asiatic home, is oblivious almost of its existence. From the middle of July to the middle of September the fair is in full swing. Then the population of Nigni-Novgorod jumps up from 80,000 to over 300,000. From every quarter of the globe traders flock to the fair, bringing Asiatic products in stones, furs, iron, and grain, which they barter for European goods. In the middle of September, by common consent, the fair closes, the traders depart their several ways, the shops are closed and padlocked, and fair-town is given over entirely to the rats until the following July.

I naturally expressed my astonishment that some use could not be made of these houses during such time as they were not used for the fair, but was informed that nobody ever thought of it—true Asiatic apathy this. Another thing, and quite as astonishing, is that for seven months the site of the fair is entirely under water. In winter the Volga rises twenty feet or more, and the whole of fair-town is submerged, the high-water mark being distinctly seen above the door-posts. One of these shops, owned by a Nigni-Novgorod trader, was opened for my inspection, and on the ground-floor, covered with rust, were several thousand pounds' worth of English gas-engines—all of which had been under water during the winter. "Surely," I said, "these goods must depreciate terribly under such circumstances? Cannot such a state of things be avoided?" The reply was characteristically Russian, "Too much trouble; besides, they'll be all right when the rust is cleaned off. Labour is cheap here."

The people of Nigni-Novgorod are optimistic, and declare that the fair will continue for many years yet. Asiatic traders dream of nothing but Nigni-Novgorod, it taking them a whole year to bring their huge stocks to the fair and take back their exchanges. The new Siberian railway may make a difference, but the Asiatic takes anything but kindly to railways, and will go on bumping his tarantass-caravans over thousands of miles of terrible roads, until the Europe-wise competitor cuts the ground from under his feet and makes him see the error of his ways.

CHAPTER XV.

BY THE SIDE OF THE VOLGA

AT Nigni-Novgorod all idea of a made road ends. Eastward there is nothing in the shape of a highway, there is only the suggestion of a trail. Although for many centuries caravans, bringing goods from all parts of Siberia and Central Asia, have journeyed to Nigni-Novgorod and to the great fair, the Government has not seen fit to lay down any sort of road over which these caravans can travel. Indeed, it has been left to the caravans themselves to find their way from one point to another. Thus, in the remote ages, a man may have found his way to Nigni-Novgorod, and the second man following to the hoof-marks of his horse may have left a little more defined trail. Then came the first "telega," which made two ruts in the vicinity of the hoof-marks, and so the roads from

Siberia and Central Asia to Nigni-Novgorod were made.

At the present time the road from the city of the great fair to Samara is but a trail, broad and marked by the wheels of many caravans and the hoofs of many horses. One cannot easily go astray so long as one keeps within the zone of those wheelmarks; but what a desert of a road it is, clay and sand, stone, and the gnarled roots of trees, a trail winding in and out of the forest or round some scarp of ugly rock, descending abruptly into valleys, climbing almost precipitous heights, crossing here and there broad and rushing streams. A country, too, almost entirely populated by Tartars and Cherimesenes, who live in a semi-barbaric manner, and are quite undisturbed by the few Russians who have had the temerity to invade their country.

I was not a stranger to this sort of road. In a previous year I had struggled over it by short and difficult stages, and realised to the full what it would mean. I set out one morning from Nigni-Novgorod with Mr. Thomas Pollock as my guide to the first station. I was well aware that Pollock would probably be the last Englishman I should see for many months, and so it ultimately proved. He accompanied me over the villainous road which I have described for twenty versts, quite sufficient for one day's work, although thirteen miles would appear ridiculous to the English cyclist. But that thirteen miles took us all day, and we arrived dead-beat at a small village, where I sought shelter and hospitality in a moujik's hut.

We had travelled so far by the side of the Volga, on the edge of a big sandstone cliff, and now and again, when the trail curved, we had caught glimpses of the broad and beautiful river flowing deep down beneath us. At the village we were surrounded almost immediately by the native population, which evinced an interest in our bicycles somewhat amusing, but an interest to be explained when I learned from Pollock that, with the exception of myself two years previously, he had no record of any bicyclist ever having been that way. Pollock lives in Nigni-Novgorod. He is captain of the only bicycle club there. He knows every bicyclist—and so he ought to know.

That night there came up the Volga a steamer, the sound of whose paddles was as music, the snort of whose siren reminded me of more civilised climes. The steamer paused at a small jetty to discharge one or two passengers, moujiks who had been down the Volga on some business or other, and to take up the one passenger who wished to go to Nigni-Novgorod—Pollock himself. There was much jabbering of voices as the ropes were cast off, and I saw the steamer back and fill and slew out into the stream; her siren going, her ports bright and glowing, one or two chinovniks in their white coats and gold epaulettes strutting the first-class deck, a crowd of moujiks in the rear, huddled together and crooning out some quaint Russian song. The beat of the paddles sounded fainter and fainter, and the sparks from the funnel grew duller and more dull. The steamer rounded a bend and was lost to sight, so there was nothing more for me to do but to walk up the long and slippery pathway leading to the village, and go back to the moujik's hut.

As I progressed slowly over this villainous road,

A FAMILY OF HAPPY TARTARS

which is known as the high road to Kazan, I met
on my way strange folk journeying from village
to village. There were Tartars, attired in their
peculiar semi-Oriental costume, with shaven pates
and round skull caps; pleasant enough people,
dignified, and not nearly so inquisitive as the
Muscovites themselves. Then there were Bashkires and Cherimesenes, the latter a Mongolian
tribe infesting the Kazan province; a wild lot
of people, but gipsy-like in their habits, strangely
inoffensive, quite timid in fact, but ugly to look
upon—almost black and almost naked. Men and
women dressed exactly alike, that is to say, limbs
swathed in cotton bandages held on by string, a
short jacket reaching just below the waist with the
breast open, exposing in the man the hairy chest,
in the woman the full bust. Tangled hair, straight,
like strings of candles hanging round the ears and
over the eyes; oblique those eyes, and flat the
nose. They would crowd around me in the villages, but deferred to me, and made way at my
slightest suggestion. Nor, as was the case with
the more truculent Russian, did they chatter
amongst themselves and laugh at my, to them,

strange costume ; but though they clustered around me they looked upon me, it seemed, with an almost reverential respect. At one small village I was forced to take refuge in the house of a " pope," or village priest. There was no post-station there, neither was there a moujik's hut where a man used to the most uncomfortable of civilised habitations would have cared to rest.

He was a priest of the Greek Orthodox Church. His house was a hut, clean it is true, consisting of but two rooms, the living and the sleeping He made me welcome, but he had only black bread to give me, and apologised profusely that he could not give me tea made from dust tea, as he had only the brick. It is a peculiarity of the priest of the Greek Orthodox Church to costume himself and arrange his hair and beard so that his appearance is suggestive of the Saviour. Many and many a time have I come across, in outlandish villages, these popes, who, by the arrangement of their hair and costume, have borne such a striking resemblance to the authenticated portraits of Christ that I have been startled. Nor can one mingle with these highly religious people without partaking in some measure of their melancholy. My stay in the house of the pope caused me but little pleasure, not that I did not appreciate the hospitality which had been vouchsafed me, but because there was that religious aspect about everything, a religious aspect so slavish, and which was so repugnant to me, that I felt glad to get away—my object, my aims, my project being so different.

I came at length to a bifurcation in the road. One way, I learned from a passing teamster, led to Kazan, the other to Samara. Here one may well pause to speculate on what distances suggest in Russia. Here was a teamster who could tell me that on the one hand there was a road to Kazan, and on the other was a road to Samara. Kazan was only two hundred miles away, Samara was only three hundred and fifty. One could speculate indeed on the English teamster who might be asked the direction to Birmingham or Leeds. It is a commentary, in fact, on the sterility of Eastern Russia. It was two hundred miles from that spot to the nearest town; it was three hundred and fifty miles from that spot to the next nearest.

So I left the Kazan track, and found myself in a country desolate beyond all description. I had got out of the zone of trees, and had left the Volga bank—the Volga which was to wind by Kazan, and reach Simbirsk and Samara by a devious route. The road I was on was now so broad that it was impossible for me to see its confines. It passed over a country devoid of agriculture or vegetation. In a sense it was a steppe, but a rolling steppe, winding and twisting over great hills. There were no telegraph posts nor verst posts; nothing to show the way, only a multitude of tracks in the sand and clay and grass. Here and there, when the track became faint, I would turn at right angles and ride until I found the deeper marks. The only method I had of knowing that I was on the right road was by sticking to the more defined wheelmarks.

In this way I progressed but slowly, for the heat was terrific. Villages were indeed few and far between, and the post-stations, now fallen into desuetude, offered practically no shelter. It was strange too to note the manner in which Tartar and Russian villages alternated. The first village would be peopled entirely by Muscovites, the second entirely by Tartars. In the one village there would be the tiny green and white church, with its glittering cross; in the next village would be the grey, flat mosque, with its stunted minaret and its crescent. On the whole I preferred the Tartar character to that of the Russians in this province, although I made it a point to sleep always in a Russian village, taking such shelter as I could get, for the Tartars were so utterly bestial, living like hogs in their miserable huts, so indescribably filthy indeed, that it were preferable to sleep in the open.

In most of the Russian villages one could find a decent *dvor* or yard, where resided the *ataman* or constable of the town. My papers were always sufficient to procure me shelter in the best houses, although never an *ataman* could read a word of his own language, but the seals and the big black eagle were enough. The desolation through all was very pronounced, while the heat was so great that I rode with extreme difficulty. But one incident served to lend excitement to this otherwise monotonous march.

It happened as I cleared through one village a small telega coming my way obstructed for the moment my passage. I was riding between two huge ruts, and in these ruts approached the cart, which was laden with hay. A woman was fast asleep on top of the hay, a man was fast asleep across the shafts of the cart. I dismounted to give them room, but the horse, frightened at the sight of my bicycle, turned, and in the twinkling of an eye the cart turned also, clean over, as a matter of fact, and the woman slid off the top at a great pace, and brought up with a thump on the hard ground. I could not see for the moment what had become of the man, but the woman in her fall had retained her hold of a long hay-rake. Seeing me, and recognising in me the cause of the catastrophe, she rose to her knees and hurled the rake at me with all her force. I stooped to avoid the missile, but it caught me on the back of the head and laid me out. The blow made me see stars and partly stunned me, so that by the time I had recovered the woman had rushed upon the bicycle, and was kicking it with her bare feet.

I was in no mood for gallantry. I went for her at once, seized her, and bowled her over just in time to turn my attention to her lord and master, who came lumbering to the rescue. I made for him, but he, probably thinking discretion the better part of valour, turned and fled. It was a highly diverting scene—the woman on her haunches screaming, her lord and master flying, the horse entangled in the wreckage of hay and cart, struggling ineffectually. I went back to the bicycle, with the philosophy that the least said is soonest mended prompting me to make myself scarce.

I met friends in Simbirsk, where two French gentlemen, doing a big business in this Volga-side city, had received notification of my intention to travel that way. Here in Simbirsk the Volga is seen at its best, a broad and rapidly flowing river, high banks amounting sometimes to respectable cliffs, a wealth of forestry on one bank, a sterile, rolling land on the other. There were a few cyclists in this town, probably half a dozen forming a club, the president of which, a baron of the Russian Empire, made me exceedingly

L

welcome, but my costume was now in a sorry state, and I was forced to decline the several hospitable invitations issued to me.

It was peculiar to notice as I went further and further from the centres of civilisation how interested people became, not only in my personality but in my journey. I was less pestered by small functionaries, and the fact that I was generally received by the head of the police was sufficient passport in itself. The whole of Simbirsk turned out to see me off. The half-dozen cyclists of the town accompanied me across the Volga, trailed with me through deep sand for ten versts, and left me to my own devices.

Samara, I learned, would take me at least four days, but for the sake of God, said everyone, "do not miss the road; there is nothing right or left of that trail, not a house—nothing!"

CHAPTER XVI.

CAUGHT IN A DUST-STORM

IN the previous chapter I have endeavoured to convey to the minds of my readers some idea of the road over which I was compelled to ride from Nigni-Novgorod to Samara. This bare, gaunt, desolate land-track seemed to me more melancholy than even the much-dreaded steppe of Baraba, in Siberia, which I had already crossed on a bicycle.

There, at least, one had telegraph-poles and verst-posts to guide one, but on the Samara track there was absolutely nothing. Added to this was the terrific heat which prevailed. Since leaving Moscow the weather (which had been winterly cold) turned completely to the reverse, and every day was brazen hot. Between Simbirsk and Samara this heat was almost insupportable.

Each day, from early morning till late at night,

the very earth was like a furnace, reflecting the hot beams sent down from a pitilessly blue sky and a fiery sun.

Sometimes while riding all the ground before me would seem to heave and rock, and over the surface waves of air could be seen. These waves were most peculiar, resembling nothing so much as the extraordinary effect given by oil upon water. They looked like gigantic webs drawn out, and radiating with all the colours of the rainbow — purple, green, crimson, and yellow predominating.

At such moments as these I was given to wonder whether what I saw was actual or whether it had been conjured up in my brain—the first effects of sunstroke. Once I was startled by seeing in the sky a Russian church upside down. It was so distinct that it seemed real. There were the cupolas and the domes, the windows, the tiny graveyard and its cluster of crosses. I could see where the green and pink wash had peeled off the walls. For a minute it trembled in the atmosphere, and then, like the passing of a rainbow, it went. A mirage, of course, and when I reached the next village I had a look at its church, but it was not the replica of the one I had seen in the sky.

One day, a day when the heat seemed to cumulate—a day when I felt that it wanted but another degree to set the earth aflame, I rolled into a small village, and, being compelled to walk through deep sand, made for the post-station. So dry was my throat I could hardly ask for milk, and to throw off my jacket and shirt and lie and pant on the bare floor of the little room in which I was seemed all I could desire at the moment.

Outside in the dusty village street the heat seemed to affect everything. Dogs lay prone on their sides; horses and oxen stood knee deep in muddy spots which were once pools; geese and ducks sheltered in the shadow; and the moujiks themselves lay like logs wherever a scrap of shadow offered some degree of difference from the blinding glare.

Looking out of the window I saw a tarantass coming slowly through the sand. The yemshik on the box was like a man asleep; his head hung down, the reins dangled loosely in his hand, the metal badge on his cap sparkled in the fierce light like gold; but everything else was dust. The horses, streaming at every pore, moved listlessly; so exhausted they seemed that they could scarcely lift a leg — in fact, they merely kicked their way along, sending up the thick black dust as they slouched through. And the passenger, an officer, in a coat which was once white, but which now showed ugly streaks where the perspiration working through had caught the dust and made it mottled.

The horses came to a standstill with a last jangle of the douga bells; the yemshik descended from his box like a man who had no heart to live; the passenger alighted, and gasped at the effort; an attendant lumbered out and lifted down a box, and, sweating, carried it in.

Half an hour later I myself ventured forth. As I gave the postmaster a few kopecs for the milk I had had, he asked me where I was going?

" To the next station," I said.

" On that? " asked he, and he shook his head at the bicycle. " And in such heat, too ! "

The village was soon left behind me, and the

rolling plain stretched away before my front wheel. I was barely out of sight of the village, when I saw something which caused me to stop and stare.

Off to the left and low down on the ground I perceived what at first looked like a big, black wave of water rolling along towards me with great rapidity. When I first saw it, it must have been at least a dozen versts away. So peculiar was this cloud that I could do nothing but stand and stare at it.

Bigger and bigger it grew, mounting higher and higher as it advanced, and as it neared I saw its billows inflected with colours of all descriptions. It spread out north and south as far as the eye could see, and now, when near in, it was sky high.

Rain, of course, I thought. But never had I seen a rain cloud like that before. In bulk it was a brownish black, but those streaks of colour which gave a lining to every billow were extraordinary and fascinating. Here I stood under the blazing sun, in an atmosphere absolutely dead calm, and there, advancing at tremendous pace, was—what?

I heard the jangling noise of tarantass bells, and looking around saw a troika tearing towards the village. The yemshik was standing on his box, shouting and lashing his horses.

This sight filled me with alarm. What could it mean? I looked at the big multi-coloured cloud and then at the troika, and then heard a low moaning sound which came from afar off, and I became filled with terror. A presentiment that something was going to happen possessed me, and seizing my bicycle I mounted with all the rapidity I could and sped back in the direction of the village.

Nearer and nearer came the cloud, now so high and sinister, while louder and louder had the moaning become. The top of the cloud bent over and circled under. Now it seemed but a verst away, and all the land beneath it was entirely obliterated. The next moment it was upon me. With a roar, a boom, the great wave enveloped myself and my bicycle. It was not rain, it was sand.

Sand of the steppe caught up in the fierce embrace of a semi-tropical gale. Instantly everything was as a seething, roaring whirlpool. I was swept off my bicycle like a straw and lay on the ground blinded, gasping and choking. I just managed to save my hat ere it was carried away for ever. To say that I was filled with terror would be to convey but a faint idea of my feelings at this juncture.

The noise, the force, and the whirl of the dust-storm were sufficiently nerve-shaking. A minute ago I had been in brilliant sunshine, and now I was enveloped in a gloom so dark as to be almost opaque, and the whole atmosphere one mass of scurrying sand.

As I lay there, scarcely knowing what to do, but all the time thinking it better to remain, something more dense than the clouds of sand came dimly towards me. It came like a ghost, for what noise it made was drowned a thousand times by the roar of the cyclone.

When it was almost on top of me I made it out to be the tarantass which I had seen just before the storm burst. The sight of it was the most gladsome of all. I rose and scrambled towards it, but was buffeted from one side to the other by the wind. I caught hold of the side of the vehicle and looked in. The two occupants were on the bottom smothered in their cloaks.

The yemshik, who kept to his box, but whose face was black and thick with dust, saw me, and whether by instinct or out of common humanity, pulled in his horses. I shouted to him, asking permission to get in his tarantass, but my voice, I think, was drowned in the noise of the wind. But I lifted my bicycle in;· I fell in myself. The two occupants, upon whom I fell, routed themselves from under their cloaks and looked at me with a frightened glare. They could not speak ; they could only look.

The horses restarted; the tarantass rocked from side to side as each buffet of the contrary winds swept upon it and threatened to hurl it over this side or that.

Minutes passed, minutes which seemed like hours, during which we crept on, and never once did the storm show signs of abatement in its fury. Then the tarantass stopped, and dimly I could see the ghostly outlines of a house on the right. The occupants of the tarantass got out and rushed to the house. I followed them. A door was opened; we entered, and the door was slammed to again.

For a moment everything was too dark to see, but presently my eyes became accustomed to the gloom. We were in a moujik's hut, and there, in the corner, before the ikon of Christ, the moujik's family, on their knees, and crossing themselves with all the fervour of religious devotion and the terror which possessed them, were praying.

For half an hour or more the cyclone continued, and then, as suddenly as it had come, it passed. A few violent blasts, as if in parting anger, and away the dust-storm reeled towards the west, a great black wave staggering along on its path of destruction.

Down from the heavens poured a flood of sunlight, lighting up with miraculous suddenness the scene which, a moment before, had been enshrouded in impenetrable gloom.

And what a scene it was now! The village street was bestrewn with timber, thatch, and the *débris* of broken and shattered huts. Dust and

sand drifts lay a foot in depth; houses were un-
roofed; a few trees, dragged up by the roots,
sprawled across the way. Heaps of hay, which
represented all that remained of trim stacks,
were scattered and bunched everywhere. Such a
spectacle of destruction I have never seen before.
Poor peasants!

Away to the west the dust-storm was getting
smaller. A great calm had settled down on the
village, a calm which, after the fierce turmoil,
seemed strange and unearthly. The hot beams
of the sun came sweltering down again, but the
rain, for which all prayed, came not.

A couple of hours later I secured my bicycle
from the post-station, where the yemshik had
taken it, and made my way once more towards
Samara, which fine city I reached two days later.

CHAPTER XVII.

ON THE EDGE OF THE KHIRGHIZ STEPPES

AND here I was in Samara, a Volga-side city which vied almost with Nigni-Novgorod in point of importance. A city doing a big trade with the lower Volga and the Caspian Sea; the junction of the great iron road leading on the one hand to Siberia, and on the other to Orenburg, a city which, when the railway to Tashkent, Turkestan, and Bokara is completed, promises to be one of Russia's most valuable centres; but a city in every other respect a replica of all the other Russian cities I had been in, and therefore without novelty—except that it was distinctly Russian.

Here I fell into good hands, for Nicolai Demtrivitch Batushkoff, the leading shipowner of the place, and *ergo* the leading cyclist, constituted

himself my adviser and chaperon. Then there
were his Excellency, the General Governor of
Samara, himself a cyclist, and Prince Galitzen,
to all of whom my thanks are due for influential
assistance in the matter of my ride to Khiva.
But of Samara itself, with its streets of houses
all at right angles, its calf-deep dust, its heat, its
semi-Asiatic languor, there is no need to speak.
Samara possesses a large number of men of
wealth, and away from the city, down by the
beautiful banks of the Volga, seven to ten versts
distant, lies Villadom, where wealthy Samarians
have their being and secure their happiness.

The Russian without his country villa, or
"datch" as it is called, is of no account. To
have a good business, to have a good income
is one thing apart; to have a "datch" on the
Volga bank seems the sum total of human
happiness. Then life rolls smoothly on. Work
is done in the stuffiness, the dust, and the blinding glare of the city, but when the sun wanes,
then from those hot streets start the troikas for
the villas, where, in the evenings, in sight of the
wonderful Volga panorama, is the time beguiled.

OPEN PAPER GRANTED TO THE AUTHOR BY THE IMPERIAL RUSSIAN
GEOGRAPHICAL SOCIETY

Visits to this "datch" or that, dinner parties, and social gatherings. Never let it be said that the moneyed Russian does not know how to live. Though the moujik in his mud-built hut may live the life of a dog, have scarcely bread enough to eat, ill-clothed and totally ignorant of anything better or of a life worth living, the other Russian, he with the roubles, has found the secret of money's influence.

Then one morning I bade good-bye to Samara, and to those who had done their best to make my short stay a pleasant one, looked for the last time on the broad waters of the Volga, and shaped my course over the hills to the level plains on the edge of the Khirghiz steppes. I had 400 versts to cover to Orenburg, and my way lay parallel with the railroad. Villages there were, but they were few and far between, so that my accommodation each night was to be the shelter of a railway station, whichever I could reach.

For the first day out I had the company of Mr. Batushkoff, who rode a hundred versts with me to the station of Marichevka. First our way lay over a broken, tumbled country bordering the

Volga, but then we plunged down into the bare and sad-looking plain which stretched away southward as far as the eye could reach. Now and again as we progressed we would come across some humble patch of agriculture or some field of half-ripened and sickly - looking wheat. Here the Russian husbandman with primitive tools would be found at work, but how one missed the hum of the steam machine, the busy clack of a British cornfield at harvest-time. Everything here in husbandry seemed to be carried on in a spiritless, half-hearted manner. Peasants grumbled at the poorness of the crop, and prayed God for better things next year. Yet God was hardly to blame, for with a wooden, shovel-like instrument for a plough which just scratched the earth to the depth of four inches, who could expect fine crops?

From Marichevka I was alone. I had hoped to make on the second day out of Samara, the little town of Buzuluk, but good fortune had deserted me. The morning broke windy and cloudy, and ere I had gone twenty versts the heavy drops of rain, heralding a storm, began to fall. On the opposite side of the road ran the railway lines, and the lone hut of a signalman peeped out from behind the embankment. I had just time to reach it before the heavy rain swashed down, and then, for the first time for five weeks, the refreshing smell of a dampened earth greeted my nostrils.

What the poor signalman thought of me when I burst into his hut, bicycle and all, and practically took possession of the place, I do not know. It is safe to say that although he had been used to the civilising influence of railway trains for some part of his life, the sight of a bicycle somewhat disconcerted him. He was not a bad old fellow, but extremely inquisitive, and wanted to know the why and the wherefore of everything in connection with both myself and my bicycle. But then, he gave me tea and milk and bread, and there I stopped the livelong day, while outside the wind howled and the rain descended in torrents. As darkness fell I made an effort to get away, but I might as well have attempted to move, unaided, the Monument. The little track of a road, hitherto dusty and hard, was now but a sea of gluey mud. My feet sank into it up to my calves and even walking was impossible.

M

Borskaia, the next station, was only a few versts away, and I did the only thing possible, and that was to drag the bicycle to the railway lines and walk over the ties to the station. The red-hatted station-master, the white-aproned porter, the white-jacketed and very pompous telegraph clerk, received me with wonder. Who was I? and where had I sprung from? But when I evinced a desire to stay amongst them, and enjoy their company, and partake of any good things which they might have about the place, and told them the oft repeated itinerary of my journey, they warmed a bit, and I was comfortable.

All the next day I remained at the station, for the road was simply impassable. To beguile the time, all I could do was to go over to some wheatfields and watch the reapers at their labour —and there is some entertainment in seeing other people work—or to wait anxiously for the train of the day, and enter heartily into the feverish bustle occasioned by that occurrence. To talk to the engine driver; to watch chinovniks bolt vodki and cucumbers; to note the pomposity and importance of the conductors; to watch the antics of the moujiks, who rode fourth-class in the cattle waggons, and then to witness the departure of the sluggish train upon its further journey.

But next day the hot sun having, to some extent, dried the railway track, I set out to ride over the narrow path which ran alongside. The road itself was still impassable. Bumping over the ties or creeping along the sandy little track beside the rails, I managed to make some progress; but how lonely and dispiriting everything was. To the right or the left was no sign of life. Off to the north a few hills melted into the horizon, off to the south the bare plain, without sign of house, of tree, or of life, lay like a ragged carpet stretching away for ever and ever; ahead and behind me were the shining metals, winding like a serpent over the surface of the earth. Once a luggage train came lumbering along, and the engine-driver hung over his box to look at me. I waved my hat to him, but he was too much interested in the strange instrument I was riding to take notice of that. Then the heat of the day began to wane, shadows crept up to the eastward, the sun went down a fiery red, and I arrived at Buzuluk to find a couple of cycling enthusiasts awaiting me and an hotel of modest pretensions, possessing a proprietor who delighted my heart by speaking German.

The ride from Buzuluk to Orenburg, a three days' stiff journey over roads which, being mere trails by the side of the railway lines, offering anything but pleasant going, brought forth no incident which is worth recording. How clear it was, however, to perceive that I was getting farther and farther from civilisation, and that soon, with the terminus of the railway system reached, I should have nothing but the Orient before me. But the ride over that sterile plain, when day after day brought no new feature, when to-day was but the replica in all surroundings of yesterday; when, mile after mile, there was nothing fresh, then was the time to think of the immensity of Russia's possessions. Such riding is not inspiriting; these steppes of Russia are more melancholia provoking than anything I can suggest. One feels so utterly lost, such a tiny atom in such a big world.

Then came the change; it was the last station before Orenburg. A little man, slightly bald, and in pince-nez, bounced in upon me. " Welcome to

Orenburg," he cried in English. "They've sent
me out to meet you; they're all waiting for you,
every one of them, and, by gad! sir, you'll have a
splendid reception." This was the advance guard
of the Orenburg cyclists, and as from the station
we made our way towards the city, whose spires
and domes were twinkling over the low hills ahead,
cyclists began to appear. We stopped at a small
garden for a drink of Russian quass, and here I
saw and talked to my first camel, the premier in-
dication of the proximity of the desert, and here
more cyclists joined us. To saddle once more,
and a goodly procession was made. Bells tinkled
and horns tootled; we rounded a bend in the road,
and the full-leaved branches of trees hung in flags
betokened a garden. Strains of military music
came to my ears, and as we wheeled down a shady
avenue those strains became plainer, and it was
"God save the Queen" that a Russian military
band was playing.

Then for a Russian welcome. To be seized by
half a hundred stalwart cyclists, chinovniks, and
others; to be tossed three times in the air as high
as human strength can throw; to have one's arms

nearly shaken off while a band plays alternately the anthems of Russia and England. Here was Orenburg, the last town of civilisation. Before me was the Kara Kum desert. Citizens of Orenburg knew that as well as I, and they meant me not to forget it.

Thanks to the good offices of Mr. Belkin, the chief editor of the *Orenburg Gazette,* and Mr. Kazachenkoff, one of the leading merchants of the city, I was able during my short stay to see much that was interesting. And no one could be aught but interested in a city which stands, as does Orenburg, like a sentinel on the edge of Europe, with all the Mohammedan world before it.

How strange to walk through these streets, to see European houses on either side, and people in European dress promenading, while down the centre trails a camel caravan, a hundred beasts strong, *en route* for the desert. Those big, lumbering beasts, each loaded with forty poods of merchandise destined for distant Bokhara, Samarcand, or Tashkent; those fantastically dressed Khirghiz, with swarthy skins and Mongolian features. Here at the back a Khirghiz

and his wife astride across a camel, their heads
bobbing backwards and forwards as the clumsy
animal slouches along.   Round the corner and we
bump into a Tartar whose round, red skull-cap
covering a shaven pate shines in the sun.   The
Tartar grunts and shambles off, to give place to
a bespurred and white-coated Russian officer,
whose cockade and whose epaulettes are of gold.
Then comes a ramshackle telega in the wake of
the camel caravan, driven by a sullen and very
ragged Bashkire, who resents the right of way
with a Russian Isvostchick, whose none-too-clean
vehicle and very shaggy pony come whirling
round the corner all sides on.   Anon will pass
a couple of Khivans whose tall, black astrakhan
hats, baggy trousers, sandals, and long silk gabar-
dines, blue, green, or yellow, give an air of
picturesqueness to the street.   Yes, here it is that
the Orient and the Occident meet.   Here the
civilisation of the West holds out its hand to the
barbarism of the East.   Here from the burning
sands of the Kara Kum come the black and
forbidding-looking denizens of the desert to barter
their wool and camel hair for tea, tobacco, and

other simple luxuries. Here hard by are great laagers where thousands upon thousands of poods of Asiatic merchandise lie in bond. Orenburg is the *entrepôt*, not so great an *entrepôt* as formerly, perhaps, for the goods of many peoples, and as such is entitled to the space which I have given it.

The General Governor of Orenburg and the General Governor of the Khirghiz Steppes have been good enough to give me open papers for the way to Khiva. I have received much good advice on all hands. None conceal the fact that I have a stiff job before me. The sands of the Kara Kum, the tiger-ridden jungles by the Aral Sea; the long, weary miles which give no water, no food, no shelter—the desert! The bicycle is ready, as sound now as when it left England; the rider is ready, thinner, and a bit more tired and more ragged than when he left England, but still ready. So good-bye to the last remnants of civilisation, and let us see what the desert is made of.

CHAPTER XVIII.

ON THE FRINGE OF THE DESERT

THE earnest German who helped me into my saddle in Orenburg whispered rather than said, "Don't ride in the night, dear sir; don't ride in the night." I had no time to ask why, since around me was a bustling crowd, a crowd composed of those who, interested or curious in my endeavour to ride to Khiva, had gathered together to see the last of one whom they, rightly or wrongly, considered to be a fool. And why not? Here at Orenburg was the end of the railway, the end of the post-track—the end of the world to these people living on the fringe of the desert. What was before me I knew not; diligent inquiry had elicited nothing more than I already knew. Over that vast desert of Turkestan lay the mist of mystery. Russian though it was, no Russian here in Orenburg could enlighten me upon its possibilities.

But for the first day at least there was nothing to render my progress any more hazardous or difficult than it had been right from London. I had company in the shape of four cyclists as far as the second station, where in the small post-house I elected to pass the night. The way had been somewhat hilly, for I was now on the foot-hills of the lower Urals, which I should have to cross ere tackling the plain. It would be idle and sheer rank hypocrisy to say that when I parted with these warm-hearted fellows I did not feel at length thrown on my own resources and further conceive the magnitude of my under-taking. Only one foreigner before me had crossed the Kara Kum desert, and he had been accompanied by guides, interpreters and escorts, and travelled in a waggon. I was alone and on a bicycle, the least practical of all methods of locomotion for such a journey.

The next day I climbed over the foothills, and for four days afterwards struggled along over a vile road, sleeping in post-stations at night and subsisting on anything but palatable food. The flaxen-headed moujik of the red shirt gave place

THE EUROPEAN-ASIATIC BORDER

THE BICYCLE CAUSES DEEP INTEREST

to black-haired, black-eyed, and swarthy-visaged
Bashkires, who were wont to gaze askance upon
me, but fortunately gave me a wide berth. And
as I went forward so my vicissitudes became
greater. When I ran out of sugar I drank my
tea without; when I ran out of tea I drank hot
water and imagined the rest. A day from Orsk
found me in a sentimental mood, and, like the
devil who was sick, I found my only solace in a
blind trust in Providence.

One day I came to the crown of a hill, and saw
away on my right the serpent-like windings of the
Ural river, and nearer in a cluster of white houses
and stumpy trees, which denoted the town of
Orsk. I rested on the crown of the hill, and a
muleteer, coming up the road, stopped his team
in order to look at my bicycle. He put some
questions to me in the Bashkire language, which
were, of course, a riddle. I replied in Russian,
and falling into my ways the muleteer asked
where I was going. I pointed south, and said
" Kara Kum." The muleteer looked gravely at
my bicycle. " On that ? " he asked, with a lift of
his eyebrows and a gleaming of white teeth.

"On that?" Then he laughed, turned to his team, said "Chu! chu!" and ambled up the mountain-side.

In Orsk I made straight for the house of the natchalnik, or head-man. My instructions from the General Governor of Orenburg had been to this effect, and in the natchalnik of Orsk I found, for a wonder, a gentleman who not only sympathised with my journey, but immediately set himself to work to help me. He told me he had already received instructions from St. Petersburg concerning me, but under no circumstances could he allow me to leave Orsk on my further journey alone.

Not only were there no towns or villages, but food was unobtainable except from the nomads themselves, and that supply could not be relied upon. Therefore, from the commencement of the Khirghiz steppe, I should be accompanied by a tarantass and three horses, which would carry all the food I should require until I reached Fort No. 1 on the banks of the Syr-daria river, whence to Khiva, across the desert, it would be necessary for me not only to take a complete caravan of camels, but also an armed escort, in order to protect me from attacks by the lawless denizens of the Central Asian wilderness.

I then obtained the necessary permission to charter a tarantass under a royal podorojania, or open paper. This paper entitled me to get horses at every post-station I came to without the least delay—an important consideration. Not only that, but I was also empowered to seize the horses of anyone coming along the road for my own convenience, paying at the rate of one and a half kopecs for each horse per verst! I bought a stock of provisions to last me for twelve days, and these, encased in a big box, were put in the tarantass. I also took with me several bottles of red wine, which I had been told would be necessary, as the water on the steppe was salt, and in places bad. My medicine-chest, which contained various remedies for possible ills, which had been forwarded on by horse from Orenburg, was also taken, as well as a flat tub of fresh Ural water. Although the whole of the way from Orsk to Fort No. 1 is under the control of the Russian Government, which has erected post-stations at stages of about twenty versts, or fourteen miles, these structures are of the most primitive description, and a traveller journeying between the two points cannot depend upon them for food, or indeed anything but boiling water with which to make his tea.

One Sunday morning I left Orsk, my tarantass preceding me, and I felt that at last I had left Russia, and left behind me, too, one of its most remarkable features. As I pedalled through the town the bells were booming out, and around the green and white church hundreds of Cossack women had assembled in their bright dresses. The vodki shops in the main street were doing a roaring trade, and moujiks, incapably drunk on the fiery spirit, lay about in all directions. This is a Sunday institution observable throughout the whole of Russia—the women go to church and the men get drunk. Vodki is the lodestone of every moujik and Cossack. They will drink it by the quart, just as the German will drink beer. Its effects are almost instantaneous, and it is frequently the case that a moujik will get insensibly intoxicated several times in one day.

The custom of the traktir proprietor, or inn-keeper, is to carry the insensible moujik very tenderly out into the street, and lay him in the middle of the road, in order to give him breathing space and time to sleep off the effects of his potations.

Crossing the Ural river the great steppe of Turkestan stretched before me. The road was frightful, dead level though the country was. Here and there I struck deep sand, through which my bicycle wheels refused to revolve, and I was compelled to dismount and shoulder the machine, while the three horses of my tarantass plunged heavily along. A couple of Khirghiz, mounted on a camel, bore me company for a short distance, endeavouring to get their unwieldy beast to race with me, but without success, until at length, disgusted, they threw up the sponge, and sheered off into the steppe. On the first day I made two stations, a distance of only about twenty-eight miles, but on the next day I found the going much better, the trail consisting of clay instead of sand. The loneliness of it all, however, soon told upon my feelings. Hour after hour I used to ride along, with nothing to be seen north, south, east, or west but one vast barren plain, with here and there a few stunted clumps of sage-brush. Once I passed a Russian moujik who was tilling a little patch of ground close to a post-station. It was a curious sight to see a European plough being used in this remote region, and more curious still to see it being drawn by camels.

For two days the road was entirely deserted, but on the morning of the third day, when we had started early on our southern pilgrimage, we met several caravans coming from Bokhara. These caravans consisted each of over a hundred camels, and here it is as well to remark that the Asiatic camel is one of the finest of the species.

It is calculated that the Asiatic camel will carry at least forty Russian poods, or over twelve hundredweight of goods on its back, in addition to a passenger. The proverb that it is the last straw that breaks the camel's back is often ex-emplified in the Turkestan camel. Forty poods is the maximum that any Khirghiz will put upon his camel; a pood above that and, as a general

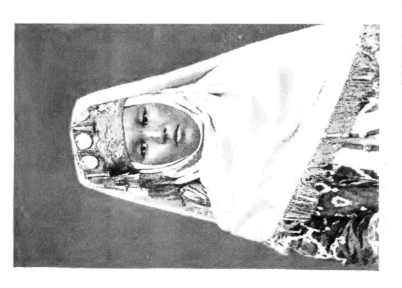

KHIRGHIZ BEAUTIES OF THE MIDDLE HORDE

rule, the camel will refuse to budge, however one may lash it.

My nights were spent in the most extraordinary places. Now and again the post-stations at which I was forced to stop were primitive to the last degree, and generally of the filthiest description. Vermin infested the very walls, and at night the floors were black with cockroaches. Already I began to realise that I was in for an uncomfortable time. Water was so scarce on the steppe that a wash was out of the question. I never took my clothes off, but preferred to sleep on a bundle of sage-brush in the open air rather than risk the terrors of the post-station. I found, however, that the staristas, or post-masters, were exceedingly obliging, but, poor fellows, they could do little to provide me with any sort of comfort.

N

CHAPTER XIX.

THE KARA KUM

ON the sixth day out from Orsk the trail ran near the shores of the Aral Sea, and for quite thirty miles I was compelled to push through a swamp, the mud and water of which reached at times over my knees. Later on we began to fall in with the Khirghiz nomads, and espied several of their kibitkas, or black tents, dotted on the steppe. Once we sought shelter from the burning rays of the sun in one of these kibitkas, and there, had it not been for the intervention of the yemshik, or driver of my tarantass, I fear my journey would have been brought to a summary end. My bicycle was looked upon with alarm and dismay, and, when I approached the encampment, the Khirghiz, mounting their horses, made for me with a rush, rending the air with their screams and shouts, and cracking their long whips in fury. Fearing that they intended to ride me down I dismounted. Along came the Khirghiz like a whirlwind, then circled around me, shouting and jabbering in a most furious manner. I threw up my hands to show that I meant them no harm, but I was not quite certain as to the better course—to draw my revolver or to submit. My tarantass was a little way behind, I could just faintly hear the jangle of the douga bells; but presently up it dashed at a great speed right into the midst of the Khirghiz, who scattered to right and left.

The yemshik stood on his box, waving his knout and shouting something in the Khirghiz language which, of course, was unintelligible to me. Anyway his presence had the effect of calming these extraordinary people, who are half Chinese, half Tartar in appearance, but as wild and reckless looking as Bashi-Bazouks. I was taken to their kibitka, and when their fears of my bicycle had been allayed and its mechanism "explained" to them they treated me kindly. Koumiss was brought and the half-raw flesh of sheep.

I was given the best position in the kibitka, generally occupied by the head-man of the tribe. A bundle of cushions was thrown down for me to sit upon. A sheepskin filled with koumiss was brought, from which I drank; and then a wooden bowl containing mutton was placed on the ground before me. There were no knives or such-like aids to eating as we have in civilised countries. I drank the koumiss from the skin, and I took up the flesh in my fingers and ate it. As soon as I had satisfied my hunger the big bowl was passed to the head-man, who ate voraciously, bolting huge pieces of meat, his eyes nearly bulging from their sockets at each tremendous gulp. After his appetite was appeased he passed the bowl on to the rest of the tribe, and like wolves they fought over the remains, gnawing the bones, licking their fingers, and generally feeding like hogs. Disgusting in their manners though they were, still I could not forget that they had given me all they had—mutton and koumiss—which constitutes practically the only food the Khirghiz has ever known.

These strange people of the steppe scarcely

THE ROAD ACROSS THE KARA-KUM

know what bread is like, and it is safe to say they have never tasted vegetables. Their greatest treats are either a piece of bread or a half-handful of tea. They make some sort of tea themselves, which they call seloni, a nauseous compound which it is impossible for a European to drink, more especially as the Khirghiz prefer it made from salt water. Koumiss, however, is rather a nice drink than otherwise. Made in the Khirghiz fashion, it is simply fermented mare's milk, and, when new, is very palatable. It has a tendency, however, to increase one's girth, and it is related that it is so nourishing that a Khirghiz can live on koumiss alone for many weeks. I have tasted so-called koumiss since I have been back in England, but it is no more like the real article than chalk is like cheese.

Passing as I now was through an extremely swampy region, the plague of mosquitoes was frightful. I carried with me a net for my head, but the heat, now that the summer was at its height, made it impossible for me to wear anything but light clothing. The consequence was that the voracious mosquitoes bit through my clothing and stung me so badly that at night it was impossible to sleep. I had to abandon, too, in this region, the idea of sleeping in the open, for it is at night the mosquitoes come out in full force. It is related that yearly many of the Khirghiz, inured as they are to the hardships of their life, perish from the mosquitoes, whilst the mortality among the horses is tremendous. It is the custom of the people at night to build huge crescents of fire made from sage-brush, into the centre of which the horses are driven, the arch of the crescent being pointed in the direction of the wind. Thus the poor suffering creatures are freed for a time from the ravaging pest, although the discomfort of inhaling dense volumes of choking smoke must be considerable.

Sleeping in the post-stations was my terror. The stings of the mosquitoes outside were bad enough, but the bites of the insects inside more than equalled them. The stench of these stations is something indescribable, and to sleep on the floor in a rug, and to feel insects of every description crawling over one's face and hands in the middle of the night, is torture of the worst kind.

Thus I struggled along at the rate of about thirty miles a day, starting at sunrise and knocking off at sundown. I had little difficulty about horses, as there were no travellers at all on the road. Naturally, my appearance on the bicycle was viewed with astonishment by the natives, and periodical attacks were made upon me, until at last I felt that unless I had some better protection than the yemshik of my tarantass, some casualty might happen. I only once had occasion to present my revolver, and that was when an unruly Khirghiz, darting out on his horse from a caravan, headed towards me with fury in his eyes and a general appearance of being bent on my overthrow. I dismounted at once, flung the bicycle from me, and sprang out of the way of the horse. It flashed by me with scarcely a foot to spare, and the Khirghiz wheeling rapidly made for me again. I at once drew my revolver, and hoping to scare him off, fired a shot in the air. What happened was the most extraordinary spectacle I ever saw. The Khirghiz reined in

his horse with such suddenness that the hind
quarters of the beast fairly rose in the air, while
the rider himself disappeared entirely from view.
He had slipped over on the other side of his
saddle, and was hanging on the neck of the horse,
and looking at me from under the bridle. Up
came my tarantass, and then explanations ensued
—a long wrangle in which my yemshik vociferated
fiercely, and kept cracking his knout as if he
would like to lay it on the other's shoulders.
After this argument the Khirghiz slouched off,
and when at a respectful distance from us sped
off to rejoin his caravan.

We now commenced to tackle the desert of
Kara Kum. The sage-brush grew scantier and
scantier, hillocks of sand appeared on either hand
—deep, fine sand, with a consistency almost like
that of flour. Our daily pace became less and
less, as I was forced to walk sometimes stretches
of ten or fifteen miles. On one or two occasions
even walking was impossible, as the sand was too
deep and the heat of it too great. My feet became
so badly blistered that I could not take off my
top-boots at night without dragging away the skin,

A KHIRGHIZ MEDICINE-MAN

and once or twice, in sheer agony, I was compelled to put the bicycle on the tarantass and ride in the equipage myself.

It was late in August when we came in sight of the oasis of Kazalinsk, on the banks of the Syr-daria river, where is situated Fort No. 1, the first of the formidable outposts thrown up by General Kaufmann during his triumphant march through Turkestan nearly twenty-five years ago. It was a delicious sight to see those tall, green trees, the long meshes of grape-vines, the tangled jungle of fruit trees, the lush grass, and the little rivulets of water running through the irrigating ditches. We entered the oasis at midday, and an hour later I had my legs under the table of the commandant of the fort, doing justice to the best meal I had had since leaving Orenburg.

CHAPTER XX.

FORT No. 1.

I HAD now accomplished the easiest portion of my Turkestan ride. The Khirghiz steppe I found to be rather better than I had expected, from what had been prophesied. The Kara Kum desert, instead of being covered entirely with sand, had rideable patches here and there; but I was promised that in the passage of the Kizil Kum desert, from Fort No. 1 to the banks of the Oxus river, the most formidable obstacles would be put in my way. The Kizil Kum, which is Sart for "desert of difficult sands," is peopled only by nomadic Khirghiz and Turcomans. There are no buildings of any description between the two points, and besides, beyond one or two brackish wells, there is no water, good, bad, or indifferent. No food is obtainable, and as for days I should have to go without seeing a single soul, it was

necessary to take everything with me from Fort
No. 1. Not only that, but there is no post-track
across the desert. Neither are there means of
defining the road without the assistance of guides,
who find their way by the colour of the sand
during the day or by the stars at night. Another
terror to be prepared for was the number of
scorpions and tarantulas which live in the sand,
and as one would be compelled to sleep upon the
ground, the prospect did not look altogether
alluring.

Again, the Russian Government, while doing all
it can to keep the Khirghiz under control, have
been unable, even in twenty-five years, to effect
much improvement in their lawless habits. To
venture alone across the desert, or even with an
insufficient escort, would mean capture, if not
destruction, at the hands of the more unscrupu-
lous; and although I did not care to go to the
rather big expense of a large caravan, the fact
was impressed upon me that unless I took a
sufficient escort the wisest thing I could do would
be to abandon the project entirely.

At Kazalinsk, therefore, I bought six camels,

and engaged the services of two Khirghiz guides, who were supposed to know the route to Khiva thoroughly. The military commander of the fort, acting under instructions from St. Petersburg, placed at my disposal three jigitas, or native soldiers, and three Cossacks, while the natchalnik, or administrator of the district, gave me the services of his own dragoman, Osman Muratr, a Khirghiz, who, speaking Russian and Sart, besides his own tongue, would act as my interpreter. The soldiers were armed with revolvers, carbines, swords, and daggers, and, in addition to my revolver, I carried with me a Winchester repeating carbine, which had been sent down by the post from Orenburg.

The purchase of the food for my caravan was the greatest difficulty, as we could form but a very indefinite notion as to how long it would take us to cross the desert. There were few records of anyone having crossed it by this particular route, as Khiva was generally approached from the south by means of the Oxus river. I was told that since Colonel Burnaby had effected his ride across the Kizil Kum, only one European had performed the same journey, a Russian geographer, who got across in sixteen days, but had suffered terribly from fever and dysentery. I purchased twelve sheep, which were to form our staple food on the march, and was told that I should be able to replenish our stock of mutton from time to time by purchase from the people of the desert. In addition I took a bag of flour for my own consumption, some dried husks, and six loaves of fresh bread. I could not obtain vegetables at all in the fort, the nearest approach being melons, of which I purchased twenty-four.

My escort, I was told, would be content to live on mutton alone, and, as it was, we found that our goods and chattels were quite enough for the six camels, when it is considered that we carried a sixteen days' supply of water for ten persons, the camels, sheep, and five horses. Of course there was the food for the horses carried, but the camels, I was told, would require nothing this side of Khiva, however long the journey took, as on the desert there is a certain amount of sage-brush upon which they can feed.

One morning we had an official parade of the

caravan, and when I saw my men all ranged up it struck me forcibly that they were the hungriest-looking lot I had ever clapped eyes on ; but it was a genial, good-humoured crowd, all the same. They sprang to my every bidding, and it seemed to me that they rather enjoyed the prospect than otherwise, since they fully expected, and rightly too, to be rewarded with a substantial present at the end of the march.

Let me have it put on record that the officials at Fort No. 1 vied with each other to render me assistance. They candidly confessed that my coming was like a ray of sunlight to them, for, situated as they are, completely out of the world, they lead a very humdrum sort of existence. Around the fort has grown up during the last twenty-five years a little colony of Russians, who trade with the desert people, bartering European goods for native work ; but this after all seems hardly worth whatever profit is made, when one takes into consideration the awful monotony of their lives.

Southward stretches the telegraph trail to the cities of Turkestan, Tashkent, and Samarcand,

THE BANKS OF THE SYR-DARIA

THE FERRY AT FORT NO. I.

but, since the trans-Caspian railroad has been
constructed, there is scarcely a passenger from
the south, the only callers at Fort No. 1 being
the native caravans on the way from Bokhara to
the north.

An excellent suggestion was made by the
natchalnik of Kazalinsk, that I should take with
me a small telega, or light native cart, which
could be tilted over so as to form a sleeping-
place for me at night, which would at least be
preferable to the bare sand. I fell in with this
idea gladly, and for a few roubles was able to
get a fairly good telega and a set of spare wheels.
This cumbersome vehicle had to be harnessed to
one of the camels, and at last, after six days'
stay in the fort, everything was ready, and I
prepared for the march. One thing, however,
I had been assured of, and that was the utter
impossibility of attempting to ride a bicycle for
the first thirty miles. The left bank of the Syr-
daria river formed a swamp for that distance,
after which the sand commenced. I should not
be able to carry the bicycle either, as the mud
was too deep and no one had ever been known

to walk through the swamp.   Necessarily, therefore, the bicycle was roped on to the back of a camel, and a small Khirghiz pony placed at my disposal for the first part of the desert ride.

We made, I think, a very imposing procession as we filed down the one street of Kazalinsk, debouched on the right bank of the Syr-daria river, and waited for the ferry-boat to take us across to the other side.   Our difficulties commenced right away.   There seemed to be hundreds of people ready to help our camels on board, but one of the wheels of the telega got smashed to splinters, necessitating a repair on the ferry.   Half-way across the river the current struck us with such force that the boat rocked dangerously.   The camels became terrified, gave utterance to their shrill nasal cries, and at length one of them fell overboard with a tremendous splash.   The "ship of the desert," as he is called, is certainly not a ship in the water.   He can swim in a way, but it is a strenuous undertaking, since the weight of his body is so great that only about an inch of his nose remains above water.   We all thought that the camel was irretrievably lost, but fortunately a small boat put out from the other side of the river, met him in mid-stream, and towed him safely ashore.

Many of the officials of the fort accompanied me to the left bank, and here a formal parting took place. A few bottles of vodki had been brought over, and the last decent meal for at least sixteen days was prepared in a kibitka erected for the occasion.

It was while waiting for the camels to be loaded, and the water-skins and barrels filled, that I saw a curious sight. An old woman, clothed in the filthiest of rags, came upon the scene. She was a Khirghiz. She carried in her arms a bundle of grass, from which she plucked incessantly and ate. She raved and threw her arms about in all directions, and I learned that she was one of the mad Khirghiz of the desert, a religious fanatic, who had sworn never to change her clothing from girlhood till death! She was an awful sight, and the less said about her the better.

I asked permission of one of the officials who accompanied me to photograph her, and this being obtained I levelled my camera upon the extra-

O

ordinary object. She saw me, screamed, and then fell on her knees in a supplicating attitude.

"She thinks you are going to shoot her," laughed the official.

The wretched woman pressed her hands over her face, cowering, shuddering, and supplicating. I got two good snap-shots, but it was some time before the woman could be convinced by the Khirghiz people around her that I had not made attempts upon her life.

A KHIRGHIZ WITCH

THE SHIP OF THE DESERT AS A CYCLIST

CHAPTER XXI.

THE START ACROSS THE KIZIL KUM

SOON after midday our caravan lined up. I mounted my horse, gave a final handshake to the good fellows who had done so much for me, and then we were off. For the first mile or two our way lay over a sandy plain, but presently we came to a depression and entered the swamp. Reeds grew in every direction, while at times we were so deep that nothing could be seen on either hand. It was a veritable jungle of bulrushes, and occasionally, owing to the restiveness of my horse, the caravan was completely hidden from me. We only kept near each other by shouts and counter-shouts. We next struck due south for a little while, coming eventually to the bank of a tributary of the river. Here a large boat, which had been sent down for the purpose, was awaiting us. We em-barked the caravan, and twelve towers set to work to drag us up the tributary as far as the water was sufficiently deep. Never have I seen men work like those Khirghiz. A long thick rope stretched from the boat and passed over each man's shoulder. The towers were most of the way up to their waists in water and sometimes up to their chins; they strained and hauled and exhorted and fumed in the most excited manner. For three hours we went on like this, when suddenly the boat grounded and we had to get out.

Night came on but found us still in the swamp. It was the greatest difficulty imaginable to get the camels along. The jigitas were repeatedly lashing them for faster pace, and now that darkness was upon us the leading strings from camel to camel and horse to horse were put up, in order that no one should go astray. At last, however, we touched dry land—a hard, sandy stretch, over which our horses frisked merrily. My dragoman told me that our first night would be spent in a Khirghiz encampment, and I should be the guest of one of the head-men of the middle horde of Khirghiz. He sent one of the jigitas in advance to inform the head-man of our coming, and I was

THE AUTHOR'S DRAGOMAN, OSMAN MURATR

THROUGH THE SYR-DARIA SWAMP

promised that in another couple of hours we should reach our destination for the day.

It is almost impossible to describe one's feelings on a desert march. The soft crunch of the sand beneath the camel's feet, the buzz and ping of numberless mosquitoes, the laboured breathing of the horses, the rattling of boot heels in the stirrups, the occasional clatter of a scabbard, the voices of the men urging on the beasts, the frequent shrill cry or snort of the camels, and the big stars gleaming down upon that waste of white sand—all make up an environment not exactly exhilarating, but awe-inspiring.

Soon we saw lights gleaming ahead. Shouts were wafted on the warm breeze, and presently we saw several brush fires burning brilliantly, and in their light the round, dome-like tents or kibitkas. Willing natives rushed towards us, and helped us out of our saddles with cries of "Yakshee! yakshee!" ("Good! good!"). I was stiff and sore from my unaccustomed equestrian exercise, and was glad, indeed, that the journey was over. A tall, handsome Khirghiz presented himself to me. He was attired in Sart costume, consisting of a long cloak reaching to his heels. On his head he wore a skull-cap made of gold and silver fibres; around his waist and binding his cloak, he wore a huge silver belt, in which he carried his whip and long native pistol. He was the chief of the tribe, and, bowing, grasped both my hands in his own, and gutturally uttered the word, " Salaam."

I was conducted to the chief kibitka, a really sumptuously decorated tent. Rich carpets covered the sand; pillows and cushions were everywhere, while the walls of the tent were decorated with trellis-work done in the most brilliant colours. There was, however, no light, except that which entered through the narrow entrance by the fires; and so I instructed the dragoman to bring a few candles from our pack. The place of honour, of course, was given to me—a bunch of pillows and cushions at the head of the kibitka. Then the chief introduced his principal wife, a tall, handsome woman, who (although the Khirghiz are Mohammedans) had her face uncovered. She was quite black; but her features, although of the Mongolian type, were much more prepossessing than were those of a more lowly order. A small boy came forward with a gourd containing water, which he poured over my hands, and presently a steaming samovar, or Russian water-urn, was brought in and placed in front of me.

In Russia, as my readers are probably aware, the samovar is a national institution. Tea-drinking in the land of the Muscovite is in every respect the most important function of the day. The average Russian will consume twenty or thirty glasses of tea at a sitting. Beyond vodki, intoxicating liquors are almost unknown; beer is seldom or never heard of except in the largest towns, and then it is mainly consumed by the foreign population. For hundreds of years tea-drinking *à la* samovar has gone on, and the system has even crept into remote Turkestan. The Khirghiz who possesses a samovar is thought to be a rich man.

A metal teapot was next brought, and, acting under the instruction of my dragoman, I ordered my own tea to be put in the pot, a compliment to my Khirghiz host. We had no sugar or milk, and drank from china bowls without handles,

instead of glasses or cups. It was extremely
awkward for me to fall into the custom of a
chief of Khirghiz, inasmuch as being the guest,
I was compelled to say " Yakshee" to everything
that was given to me ; nor would anyone attempt
to eat or drink until I had first tasted the viands
or liquids.

I drank a bowl of tea, and, still acting under
instructions, said "Yakshee," whereat my host
nodded, smiled, poured out a bowl for himself
and drank it. We drank the whole contents of
the samovar before food was brought. I understood that one of our sheep had been killed and
the flesh was being cooked. Presently a rough
wooden dish was brought and laid before me.
On it were the heart, liver, kidneys, and other
tit-bits which had been spitted and roasted over
the sage-brush fire. Once again the small boy
came along and washed my hands. I tucked
up my sleeves and, seizing the heart, gnawed at
it in what I considered to be the true Khirghiz
style. I ate to repletion, for I was hungry, then
passed the dish to my dragoman, who immediately handed it to the chief, who so far had

watched me with eyes dancing with delight at my appetite. The chief ate, and the dish was then handed to the dragoman, and so it went on until all was finished.

A little later a huge bowl of broth, made by boiling the other parts of the sheep, was brought in. I drank from it first, and then it was passed round in the orthodox manner.

Then the remainder of the sheep, boiled to a nicety, was brought in and placed, just as it was, on the mat. I had already eaten enough, but rather than appear anything except accustomed to Khirghiz etiquette, I picked various pieces of flesh and ate them, and so the whole sheep disappeared, being handed from one to the other according to rank and distinction, until the residue fell to the lowliest of the crowd, and the scramble, which I have previously described, took place.

Nothing could exceed the courtesy and attention which were paid to me. My slightest wish was interpreted from a look, and when, after the feast was over, more tea was brought, and I broached a bottle of vodki (of which, however, I could not induce any of the Khirghiz to par-

take, since they are Mohammedans), I felt that
if this was the frightful discomfort of travelling
across the desert, exaggeration should be laid to
the credit of someone.

I did not know, however, that this little orgie
had been previously arranged by my friends at
Fort No. 1, and I certainly did not know what lay
before me on the desert of Kizil Kum.

A Khirghiz, attired in the usual flowing robe
and furry hat, next came in and sat cross-legged
in front of me.   He had with him a guitar-shaped
instrument with two strings, from which he
strummed a weird and unearthly air.   Then his
voice went out in a wailing song, altogether indescribable, but nevertheless not unpleasing.   We
smoked *papiros* and listened to him for some
minutes, when he rose and, with many salaams,
backed out of the doorway.

Then came the ablutions and the devotions of
the Khirghiz, and throughout the small encampment the wail of "Allah! Allah! Akbar!" resounded on the still air, mingled with the shrill
cries and sneeze-like cries of the camels, the neigh
of the horses, and the yelping of dogs.

THE HOSPITABLE KHIRGHIZ

MUSIC IN THE KIBITKA

CHAPTER XXII.

TROUBLE WITH THE BODYGUARD

OSMAN, my dragoman, awakened me at sunrise, and by the time I had consumed a couple of bowls of tea the camels had been packed and the caravan made ready for the start. I was told that with ordinary luck we ought to do at least sixty versts, or forty miles, that day, as there was very little deep sand. Having got my bicycle ready, Osman mounted his horse, and we set off in advance of the caravan, preceded by one of the Khirghiz, who was to show us the way for a few versts. Leaving the encampment, we passed a few women who were milking the mares in order to make koumiss; and I was astonished and delighted to find most excellent going soon after we got off the little plateau of stubble-grass surrounding the encampment.

There was not a trace of loose sand anywhere; the whole surface was as hard as concrete, this, I understand, being a kind of crust left by the rains of the last wet season. Underneath this crust, which was about an inch thick, the soft sand lay to a depth of several feet. It was a most extraordinary sensation to ride on this surface, as the wheels crackled over it, and I could see it waving here and there just as thin ice does under a skater. It was, in fact, the smoothest surface I had ever ridden on, being levelled by nature, and without the slightest sign of rise.

Poor Osman and his horse were soon completely outdistanced, although they strove might and main to keep up with the "devil's tarantass," as Osman himself facetiously called my bicycle. The astonishment of my escort at the machine may be well imagined when it is explained that not only had they never seen such an instrument before, but had never even heard of it; and after we had gone some five or six miles, and waited for the caravan to come up, I feel sure that the members of my party looked upon me as a sort of magician. It was impossible to explain to them how I kept my equilibrium, and when one of them tried the machine, and came off with a sounding thump on the hard ground, it was generally voted an instrument which no true Mohammedan ought to have anything to do with.

We progressed steadily until midday, when the heat became so unbearable that I called a halt. The little tent which we carried with us was rigged up, and in this I sought shelter, whilst the two guides searched for a few dried roots of sage-brush to make a fire and prepare some tea. It had been my plan when I left Kazalinsk to share and share alike in everything with regard to food, and I had given instructions to Osman to see that everybody had his fair share. If I had known what complications would ensue through this arrangement I would never have made it, but I knew nothing then of the various grades in which these men hold themselves. For instance, none of the Cossacks would collect wood for the fire. Neither would they help in the unpacking of the camels, as there happened to be with them two Khirghiz of lower caste (the guides); and upon these two poor fellows it seemed that the whole work of the caravan was devolving.

Osman, too, in spite of the alacrity which he had displayed at the beginning of the journey, turned out to be an insufferably lazy fellow.

Moreover, once out of sight of the last traces of civilisation, he became too friendly for my liking. However, I suffered all this without demur, waiting for my opportunity to assert my mastery over the caravan.

As soon as the sun had declined a little we set off once more, and through the whole afternoon I had the pleasure of riding over an excellent surface, while here and there it was possible to trace the track of previous passing caravans in a shallow depression of the concrete-like surface.

Night came almost as soon as the sun went down. The tent was pitched when the caravan arrived, tea was made, the camels turned adrift to grub for themselves for food, and the horses fed and watered ; there being adjacent a fairly large well of water, which, although too strongly impregnated with alkali for human consumption, was good enough for the animals. Our meal that day was much the same as we had had on the previous day, namely, mutton. I had, however, grown tired of the mutton, and asked for the flour, so that I could make a hot cake or "damper," as the Australians call it. Judge of my surprise when it was announced that the flour could not be found anywhere. It had either been lost on the road or stolen by the friendly Khirghiz with whom we had spent the previous night.

The bread which we had brought with us was very hard, and although we had been only two days on the march I was concerned to find that it was already getting mouldy—this, no doubt, on account of the slack baking and the heat which we had been passing through.

It was after the meal was concluded that I went outside the tent for a breath of air, leaving Osman and the three Cossacks in possession of the remainder of the feast. Lifting up the flap of the tent I nearly fell headlong over someone who was lying across the doorway. Looking down I perceived him to be one of the guides. The poor fellow crouched out of my way in supplicating attitude, and then, raising himself upon his knees, said something to me in a half-whisper, which, of course, I could not understand. He perceived this, and shook his head in a sorrowful manner. His companion then joining him, pointed to his mouth and rubbed his stomach, signifying that he was hungry—a pantomime which I easily understood. Of course, I thought they were simply hungry for the remainder of the mutton which my escort was now busily engaged upon; but one of the guides pointed to the sky and swept his arm round in a circle until the digit-finger came to the sky again. Then round went his arm again until the finger again fixed itself in the direction of the sky. It took me a second or two to puzzle this out, but at length the idea flashed upon me—the poor wretches had had nothing to eat for two days.

I was furious with anger, and, going back into the tent, upbraided Osman in no measured terms. He admitted that it was probable the guides had had nothing to eat, but it was nothing to do with him how two dirty Khirghiz got their food. The Cossacks should have seen to this. The Cossacks denied the responsibility, asserting that it was the duty of the jigitas to see that the guides were fed. In their turn the jigitas knew nothing about the matter, and looked in open-mouthed astonishment at me as I stood in the middle of the tent speaking in my broken Russian to Osman.

Seeing that it was necessary to take the bull by the horns at this juncture, else I should not have my way at all for the remainder of the journey, I took the whole of the remaining portions of the meat from the Cossacks, who had been gorging like wolves, and taking out my knife, divided it into equal parts. I then called in the two guides and gave them their share. Never have I seen fellows so grateful as they. Osman and the Cossacks looked black and sullen, but it was clear that even if I had made myself a little unpopular, I had at least asserted my authority in the matter.

From that day forth, however, I found that not only had I difficulties in the way of the heat and sand to contend with, but on my shoulders also fell the responsibility of keeping my caravan in working order. Fortunately I had good maps with me, but, excellent as they were, they were very unreliable, and, although I took frequent observations for my latitude and longitude, I could not make them agree with the trail marked upon the Russian map.

I found too that the Cossacks were beginning to

P

deceive me in regard to distances—not that I believe they knew much about the journey. We calculated that on the third day out we ought to do at least sixty versts, or forty miles, and, on measuring up the map and allowing ten per cent. for wandering off the track, I calculated this should bring us to the first well in the desert. I mentioned the matter to Osman, but he said that would be an impossibility, as the well was two days' journey off.

"Then," I said, "we will do sixty versts to-day whatever comes, and at midday will rest only half an hour for tea."

"But, Barin" (one of noble birth) "we cannot go on all day with only one drink of tea!"

"You have water with you," I said, "and that is enough; that is all I take, and I have to ride a velocipede. We start at sunrise."

Since grumbling had started in the camp, I fully determined to hold my own, knowing how vital was the necessity of getting forward, for we had only provisions and water enough for sixteen days. If it took more than that starvation would stare us in the face, unless we should fall in with some friendly tribes to replenish our larder.

IN THE DEEP SANDS

A MIDDAY HALT

CHAPTER XXIII.

A BRUSH WITH THE KHIRGHIZ

ON the next day the good surface ended, and long before midday I found myself plunging blindly along through knee-deep sand, with scorpions darting about in all directions, and Osman riding by my side with a half-jeer, half-smile on his face at my strenuous efforts. Several times I was forced to rest, and on one occasion I got stuck so deeply in the sand that it was impossible for me to move. I had to be lifted almost bodily out of it, and for another five or six versts rode on the top of a camel with my bicycle dangling at my side.

The work of getting the telega through this stuff was stupendous. The sand came right over the tops of the wheels, and the whole of the caravan had to be harnessed to the little cart, dragging it through the sand, sometimes on its sides, and sometimes on its wheels. It looked like nothing so much as a snow-plough in full swing.

Hard ground was reached again soon after midday, and here we pitched our camp and consumed a few bowls of tea. It was delightful once more to feel the wheels spinning smoothly beneath me, for my first experience of camel riding was far from pleasant, as all those who have tried this method of locomotion will readily understand.

That night, the third on the desert, the announcement was made that the bread had gone entirely rotten, and would have to be thrown away. I fancied, too, that the tea tasted somewhat peculiar, and going to one of the water tubs was convinced that the water had begun to smell. Osman, who was a little brighter and more cheerful since yesterday's episode, endeavoured to put the best face on the matter, saying that at the well of Bia-Murat, four days hence, we should be able to replenish our stock. I was even thus early in the march feeling far from well. The terrific exertions, combined with the great heat, were beginning to tell upon me. I became feverish and hysterical, and only by liberal doses of quinine could I that night compose myself to sleep.

The fourth day went by without any incident, except that we fell in with a band of roving Khirghiz, who swept down upon us and were all around us in a moment, just as if they had dropped from the skies. They came to beg tobacco and tea, but we had none to give them, and they went away disconsolate, hurling shouts at us as they went. Here Osman came out in his right capacity. To be insulted by dirty, wandering Khirghiz was not to be suffered without resentment. He ordered up the three Cossacks with stentorian cries of " Skoro! skoro!" and bade them pursue the Khirghiz and inflict chastisement.

The Cossacks went off like shots from a gun, the horses scattering the sand right and left, and the riders' faces low down to escape the wind. They went across the intervening distance between themselves and the Khirghiz like meteors, their long knouts cracking in the air as they swept along. Then came one of the most interesting sights I have ever seen. Perceiving the Cossacks were after them, the Khirghiz turned tail and fled. They made their horses double and redouble, endeavouring to elude their pursuers, but the Cossacks were too smart for them. They singled them out one by one, and gave them a sound trouncing with their whips, and in one instance a Cossack plucked one of the offending Kirghiz from his saddle, and, holding him by the neckband of his long coat, dragged him along in the sand until, with a gesture of disgust, he flung him with his face to the earth. Not for one moment did the Khirghiz endeavour to resent this onslaught; the big brass plates on the breasts of the Cossacks prohibited any retaliation.

The next two days passed without incident, and I was looking forward eagerly to the well of Bia-Murat, which marked the half-distance stage across the great desert. The first half, I was told, was the easiest, as beyond Bia-Murat the sand lay deeper, and there was little sage-brush with which to kindle a fire. We came one night upon a Khirghiz encampment, where the head-man gave us the shelter of a sumptuous kibitka, and where the best sheep was killed to mark the occasion.

Our commissariat was now dwindling considerably, and I began to see the force of husbanding some of the luxuries, such as the melons and the tea. The order announcing this was received sullenly enough by my escort, whom I firmly believe would have eaten everything we had in a day if they had had the chance. Each day, too, I took upon myself the duty of seeing that everybody had a fair and equal share of everything on the board—guides, jigitas, Cossacks, and "ourselves"—in which I include Osman and myself. The work of getting across was equally hard for everybody, and it was not the sort of environment, so at least it seemed to me, to stand upon ceremony or questions of caste.

I am firmly of opinion that had I not adopted this course we should never have got across the desert in the time we did. One day when I had been riding with Osman over a flat stretch, we waited for several hours for the caravan to come up. Osman began to fear that we had got off the track, and that the caravan was ahead of us. I was of a different opinion, however, as, according to calculations, I knew we had come in an exact south-south-east direction, and as we could see for at least three miles on either hand, there was no question of our being off the track.

I told Osman to wait where he was, and without

reluctance he consented to do so, while I sped back in the direction I had come. What was my astonishment, after a ride of about five miles, to see my caravan " in laager," so to speak! The tent was up, a fire was blazing, and, lo and behold! there were my faithful Cossacks, jigitas, and guides indulging in an orgie of melons and the only bottle of brandy I had with me. I came upon them with a silence and suddenness which nearly paralysed them. Jumping from my machine, I was amongst them in a moment, the bottle of brandy was snatched from the hands of one of the Cossacks, a piece of melon was knocked out of the fist of another fellow, and a hearty kick given to one of the lazy guides before a word had been uttered on either side.

Not a man, of course, could understand what I said, but my looks were enough. They slunk away utterly abashed and discomfited at my appearance. The camels were repacked, the tent brought down, and off the whole lot plodded again until we reached Osman, who was comfortably asleep on the hot sand.

That night melons were out of the bill of fare. One of the Cossacks brought a melon and placed it before me with a smirk, and, after spitting on the knife and rubbing it on his sleeve, handed me that instrument also. I carefully cut up all the mutton that was brought in and shared it out, and after it had all been eaten covetous eyes were cast upon the melon.

"Tell them," I said to Osman, "to take it back and put it in the bag."

Osman looked at me as if thunderstruck.

"Tell them," I repeated, "to take it back and put it in the bag."

He gave the order, and the melon was replaced. I began to feel now that I was getting my little company into something like order, for the next day they were ostentatiously polite in everything they did.

I felt so queer at our evening meal on the seventh day out, that I could eat nothing, although it had been twenty-four hours since food passed my lips. None of my escort, however, would deign to touch a morsel until I had eaten something. I protested that I was not well, and could not eat, and bade them go on. They waited for quite an hour before they would touch anything, and at last one of them came to me with the suggestion that they were all very hungry, and if I would only eat a piece of salt they would gladly fall to according to my permission.

On the eighth day a long caravan hove in sight, as well as a party of Khivans riding on donkeys. These were the most extraordinary people I had ever seen. They were fine men—tall, muscular, and as black as negroes. Their costume was savage in the extreme. Each man was armed with knives and pistols, but their headgear, consisting as it did of an enormous black sheepskin bonnet or shako bigger than a grenadier's busby, gave them a most ludicrous appearance—more especially as they rode donkeys so extremely small that the men had to curl their legs up under the bellies of the beasts to prevent them dragging in the sand. The Khivans informed us that the well of Bia-Murat was now only half a day's journey, and if we pressed forward we should reach it that night. They wound up their information with supplications for tobacco and tea, which I was forced to refuse, in spite of the munificent offers of snuff which were made on the part of the donkey riders.

KIBITKAS AT THE WELL OF BIA-MURAT

CHAPTER XXIV.

THE WELL OF BIA-MURAT

OSMAN and the Cossacks were for making Bia-Murat on the next day, suggesting that the horses were played out, and, poor beasts, there was no question about that, for they hung their heads and dragged their steps in a most miserable manner. As for the camels, they seemed to be as blithe and springy as they were when they started, though they had had nothing to drink for five days, the last time being on the morning when we left our first desert encampment. I would not, however, consent to another night without fresh water, for ours had become positively awful. It was so bad, indeed, that when we made tea the compound turned almost as black as ink, and the sugar which I was wont to put in the concoction would not sink to the bottom until it had become completely saturated.

219

What was the matter with the water I could not tell. It was not salt, nor did it exactly stink, but there was a musty, earthy flavour about it which I had never experienced before.

There were shouts of gladness late that same afternoon when away in the distance we saw fires blinking on the desert, and knew that in an hour or so we should have reached the half-way stage. The Cossacks and jigitas spurred forward their jaded horses, and I, having a clear run on hard sand, made a race of it. Queer as I was I easily got in first, to the profound astonishment, not to say terror, of the half-hundred or more Khirghiz who were encamped around the well.

Our caravan, it seemed, was expected, and I was astonished at this, until Osman made the revelation that the commander of Fort No. 1 had telegraphed to Fort Petro-Alexandrovsk by way of Tashkent, Samarcand, and Bokhara, to send out someone to see me over the remaining stages of the journey.

That night was one almost of revelry, for here not only were we able to replenish our water tubs and skins, but we were able also to purchase

THE AUTHOR GETTING USED TO KHIRGHIZ LIFE

THE WELCOME WATER

a few more sheep. The Khirghiz women super-
intended the culinary arrangements, while willing
hands took the horses and camels down to the well.

Bia-Murat, it seemed, was a sort of permanent
station, for there were several families who lived the
whole year round on the spot. Some possessed
splendid kibitkas, but others only had the shelter
of primitive rush and reed huts.

I was astonished to learn that Osman and the
escort were going back from this point, and that
forward to Khiva I should be accompanied by
one Khalibi Bekel, a Bokharan in the service of
the Russian authorities at Petro-Alexandrovsk.
This picturesque individual, who was a man of
about sixty years of age, spoke not a word of
Russian, and he had with him four truculent-
looking Khirghiz, who were to act as my escort
in place of those who were to return to Fort
No. 1. Remembering the trouble which I had
had with my original bodyguard, I looked upon
my new companions with no sort of favour.
They were a dirty-looking lot of desperadoes,
armed to the teeth, and with a demeanour sullen
and uninviting. There was no help for it, how-

ever, so I had to make the best of the situation. I was glad that we had been able to replenish our stock of provisions, and I learned with some degree of satisfaction that, all being well, we ought to reach the oasis of Petro-Alexandrovsk in six to seven days, or one or two days earlier than I had ever hoped.

It was at the well of Bia-Murat that I saw an interesting Khirghiz ceremony, namely, the method of curing the sick amongst the nomads. Osman brought me from my tent and took me along to one of the kibitkas of the Khirghiz. An extraordinary spectacle then presented itself to me. Outside the doorway of the kibitka lay a man writhing in agony. Behind him, and sitting on his haunches, was one of the ugliest and most repulsive individuals I have ever seen. Osman described him as the doctor. This fellow had a huge instrument with two strings, upon which he continually strummed, chanting all the time in a doleful manner, and winding up the end of each verse of his song with a piercing shriek.

The man on the ground was attacked by dysentery, and this, I was informed, was the method by which the Khirghiz were cured. When the doctor had got half-way through his song, a couple of Khirghiz approached, carrying two sheep. One was placed at the head and the other at the feet of the patient, and at a given signal each Khirghiz whipped out his knife and cut the throat of the animal, so that the blood should fall on the head and feet of the man to be cured. Whether it cured him or not I do not know ; but, disgusted with the spectacle, and partly fearing that the man was suffering from an infectious disease, I went back to my tent.

Osman informed me that this was the sole method of cure which the Khirghiz adopt. They have no idea of medicine, and it was quaint to hear my dragoman's answer to my query as to what happened when a man fell ill.

" He dies," said he, " simply dies."

Next morning my caravan, sadly travel-stained, was got ready. Osman and his companions brought forth their horses, and, hard as I had been on them during the journey forward, I could not help a little sentimental feeling for them in their journey back across the Kizil Kum. I gave each man a money present, and to Osman himself a gold-embroidered skull-cap, with which he was more than pleased, and after hand-shaking in the peculiar Mohammedan fashion, we parted, they going to the east and we to the west.

For the first time I was now unable to converse with anyone. Bekel was a decent old fellow, trotting by my side and looking with profound awe upon my bicycle. The four men forming the escort accompanied the caravan to shield it from any raid on the part of wandering Khirghiz or Turcomans, for I now learned that we had passed over the zone of the Turcoman tribes, and should have to be very wary. Although Bekel knew not a word of Russian, it is strange how two men in such a condition as he and I were able to understand each other; and although the first day passed without any incident worth recording, it cemented our friendship, while I was gratified to find that my Mohammedan bodyguard were my abject slaves, refusing not only to eat with me, but also refusing to share the tent at night, preferring, probably out of respect to myself, the sands outside.

A STRANGE METHOD OF CURING THE KHIRGHIZ SICK

I now began to find the way extremely difficult. Again and again I was compelled to take to the camels. I frequently plunged on through the deep sand as far as possible, and that was as far as nature would allow me. I began to realise, also, that I was getting extremely weak, since I could not walk through the sand with the same vigour which I had felt at the start of the desert march. The least bit of sand discouraged me terribly, and I got into fits of despondency from which it was difficult to recover.

On the second day from the well of Bia-Murat we entered a country composed of huge hillocks of sand, some of them twenty or thirty feet high. I can compare the sight to nothing so much as a swelling sea suddenly petrified. The hillocks were wave-shaped, with ripples of sand all over them. On every hand not a shrub or bush was to be seen —nothing but this blinding white sand, scorching hot, and into which one sank over the knees. It was difficult, too, for our guides to find their way, and one used to go in advance of the caravan and pilot us along by his shouts. He was very frequently at fault himself, however, and on

Q

several occasions we made long detours before the right direction could be ascertained.

On that day, too, an incident occurred which might have terminated in a far more tragic manner than it did. I had got ahead, not only of the caravan but of Bekel, and, wearied with my exertions, lay down on the sand. I think I must have fallen asleep, but I certainly do remember picking from my face what looked like an enormous spider. I thought nothing of it until I began to feel a pain underneath my left eye similar to that left by a mosquito sting. In ten minutes my cheek had become enormously swollen, and it was clear to me that I had been stung by some reptile or other. By the time Bekel came up my face was swollen so much that I could not even see out of the left eye. As soon as Bekel saw me and noticed my face he seemed stricken with terror. He leapt from his horse, knocked rather than pushed me down, and with the fingers of both hands commenced pressing the protuberance which had grown under my left eye. The pain was terrible, and I yelled in my agony, until I think I must have fainted—although I well remember one of the Khirghiz coming with a long knife, when at once the idea entered my brain that they intended to kill me.

The knife, however, was only used to extract the sting of a tarantula, which had bitten me. It was not until I reached Petro-Alexandrovsk, and related the incident to the doctor of the lazaret there, that I understood that it was to the promptitude of Bekel and the Khirghiz that I owed my life. Another hour and it would have been too late.

Our first encounter with the Turcomans occurred on the fourth day from Bia-Murat. I was now in such a weak condition that bicycling was completely out of the question, especially as we were passing over sand so deep and hot that to venture the foot upon it meant raising blisters all over the skin. It is a well-known fact that in this particular part of the desert the sand gets so hot that eggs can be roasted in it in less than two minutes. How the horses and the camels stood it is beyond my comprehension, but stand it they did, with never a whimper.

Our halts became much too frequent for my

liking. The slightest excuse was taken advantage of for tea-drinking on the part of my escort, and considering the heat this was not to be wondered at. Nevertheless it was a dull, monotonous plod, plod, plod, every man of us realising that our only hope lay in getting forward, and that every step made was one nearer to the goal. It was about mid-day, and I was sitting in the little tent drinking some wine, for I had now abandoned tea entirely, when one of the Khirghiz came in with a shout, "Turkmen, Turkmen." Up jumped Bekel, and I after him. I heard shouts and cries, and the loud cracking of whips, but for a moment could see nothing but a blinding cloud of sand. In a few seconds, however, I perceived a band of horse-men swooping down upon us, and before I knew exactly what was the matter we were surrounded. Bekel and his men were already on horseback, and a lively time set in. The Turcomans, attired in the Bokharan costume of huge turbans and long cloaks, were armed to the teeth, and the chief of them, a black, villainous-looking fellow, rode straight for the tent. Bekel, however (plucky old man), went for him without any ado. He

A SUMPTUOUS KIBITKA

THE LAST WELL ON THE DESERT

slashed his whip in the air, and at the same time caught hold of the chain around his neck, which supported his breastplate. The Turcomans drew near and inspected the plate; there was a hurried consultation, and then, with a shout and a confused scattering of sand, they careered out of sight.

The all-powerful influence of Nicholas II., Emperor of all the Russias, then came home to me; that these savages should respect and bow to the brazen emblem of his authority was to me an object-lesson not easily to be forgotten.

CHAPTER XXV.

PETRO-ALEXANDROVSK AT LAST

THE next day occurred an adventure which I look upon as being the most serious of the whole arduous journey across the desert. Soon after midday we got clear of the deep sand, and I was overjoyed to find a hard surface upon which I could ride. The bicycle was taken down, and I was soon speeding merrily over the crackling ground, accompanied by Bekel, who cantered on his horse at my side. We paused at intervals in order to allow the caravan to catch up, and now that the road was so good I suggested, in panto-mime, to Bekel that we might do at least another ten versts that day, for I realised that every verst less was something to be thankful for.

Night came on and found us still on the march. Bekel and I had got considerably ahead of the caravan, but I was assured that he knew the way.

By the time that the moon, now in its last quarter, rose I calculated that we were at least five miles ahead, and suggested a halt, but my companion shook his head and still cantered on. Feeling sure that he knew his road I made no demur and kept on. We ultimately pulled up at what looked like a deep gulch, rendered all the more forbidding by the uncertain light of the moon. Bekel dismounted, crept down this apparently deep chasm, and I followed, carrying the bicycle on my shoulder.

Reaching the other side we set off once more, but in about five minutes' time Bekel called a halt, and said something which will always remain a mystery. Anyway he dismounted from his horse and began searching the ground, which was now completely lighted by the moon. The conviction came home to me then that he had missed the trail and was searching for it. Presently he waved his hand to me, and, remounting his horse, set off in an entirely different direction from that which we had been following, going straight in the path of the moon. I followed him, and for at least half an hour we kept on a straight course, with no interruptions except small patches of sand and occasionally thickets of sage-brush. At the end of this half-hour my dragoman once more dismounted, waved his hands in panto-mime, and gave me to understand that we were off the trail.

Not unnaturally I was angry at this ; but what was to be done ? We had arrived at the edge of a sand-drift, and I knew how impossible it was to get through that with my bicycle. Still, Bekel was quite unconcerned. He got his saddle-cloth off his horse, spread it on the ground, and knelt down to pray. Meanwhile I stood over him, praying in a very different kind of way. His invocations to Allah being finished, he con-tentedly curled himself on his mat, and in a few moments was wrapped in slumber.

This was, indeed, a nice predicament, more especially as I was famished, having had nothing to eat for over twenty-four hours. The pain of my eye, too, was excruciating, and I was utterly wearied in body and mind. I sat down on the edge of the saddle-cloth to survey the scene. Nothing but a boundless wilderness on every hand, the only object in this sterile plain being the horse, which sent out its long black shadow on the dazzling white sands. The only sounds that broke the awful stillness were the crunching noise of the horse's hoofs, the heavy breathing of my companion, and the scuttling of the lizard-like reptiles that seemed to be in their millions in the sand.

I strove hard to keep awake, but could not, and slept as I sat—how long I do not know; but I awoke with a start under the impression that I had heard something. It sounded like a bell, but when I was fully awake I could hear nothing. I was preparing to doze again when I again heard the sound of the bell, and, getting up, looked eagerly in every direction. For many minutes I could see nothing, but presently, silhouetted against the sky-line, I saw a long train of camels creeping slowly forward.

I roused my companion at once. He grumbled and grunted, but, running for his horse, soon mounted, and we commenced to struggle in the direction of the caravan, shouting as we went. I fired a couple of shots in the air to attract the attention of the camel drivers, and was gratified to see that the train was brought to a halt. It was our own caravan, sure enough, and whatever might have been the gratification of Bekel, I know that mine was intense. Out there in that wilderness it seemed like coming upon a town to see our train of horses and camels and the poor, battered telega once more.

Whether it was owing to this upset, or to the exposure, I do not know, but that night I was in a high fever and became delirious. I understood afterwards that our caravan had fallen in with some Bokharans, who were making their way to Fort No. 1, but I have no clear recollection of anything until the next day, when I found myself on a camel and within sight of the last well before Petro-Alexandrovsk.

It was not until that night, when I had somewhat recovered from my fever—a recovery due solely to liberal doses of quinine—that I found I had been robbed of my pocket-book, while several of the little luxuries I had brought with me were lost for ever. In my condition, and realising that we were so near succour, I made no complaint, as the last thing I now desired was to raise the ire of my escort. I was in no fit state even to endeavour to assume the mastery of the whole arrangements as I had been earlier on the desert march, but allowed things to drift on. Indeed, until we came in sight of the oasis of Petro-Alexandrovsk, which occurred on the fourteenth day of the journey, I have no clear recollection of what happened. I was in a high state of fever, my clothing in rags, and, so far as my memory goes, I must have been delirious. The Khirghiz, although inured to the desert life, were, if not quite so bad, at least sullen, dogged, and unwilling to do more than they could possibly help.

The last day was a frantic scramble. We had only forty versts to do, and I felt strong enough to ride the bicycle. I noticed now that we were gradually leaving the sand, for here and there patches of green, instead of grey, sage-brush appeared, indicating the proximity of earth. We halted for a brief space on the edge of the oasis, and erected our tent in the quickest way possible, so anxious were we all to get forward. We were quickly away again, and presently the trees near Petro-Alexandrovsk were sighted, and soon we left the last of the burning sands of the Kizil Kum and entered the oasis. My escort, indeed, seemed to appreciate their arrival even more than I did; in fact they were frantic with delight, and capered like monkeys when we touched the first grass.

Peculiar mud huts next made their appearance. Swarthy Khivans, dressed in their extraordinary costumes and wearing great sheepskin bonnets, came down to us, and a long palaver was held.

Melons, figs, and other semi-tropical fruits were brought down in abundance, and a "Beg," or head-man of a section of Khivans, beseeched me to partake of the hospitality of his house, which was adjacent. I was, however, very anxious to get on to the fort; but rather than disappoint the hospitable Khivan, we entered his mud-built house, which seemed, after fourteen days' wandering on the desert, a veritable palace to me. Tea was made, and some flat cakes of bread, something like oat-cake, were given us. The Beg himself was profoundly astonished at the bicycle, and could not take his eyes off it.

THE LAST DESERT ENCAMPMENT

THE WALLS OF KHIVA

Later in the day we continued our journey to the fort, a distance now of only ten versts. We passed many fields under active cultivation, whilst I was astonished to see the number of irrigating ditches stretching in every direction.

Let it be understood that, although the oasis of Petro-Alexandrovsk is rich with fruit and cereals (there is scarcely a foot of ground uncultivated), it is all owing to an irrigating system commenced centuries ago by the primeval inhabitants of Khiva. For nine months of the year not a spot of rain falls, not a cloud is to be seen, and it is clear to me that the right bank of the Oxus river was a desert right up to the delta, but that the ground now occupied by Petro-Alexandrovsk has been reclaimed from the sands by a system of irrigation which is as complete as it is marvellous, considering the state of the country and the condition of its inhabitants.

The ten versts to the fort were soon reeled off. I presently heard the cheerful blare of bugles in the distance, and it was a glad sight indeed to see a battalion of white-coated Russian infantry swinging along the road to a stirring bugle march. Crossing little bridges over the irrigating ditches, we ultimately reached the vicinity of the fort, around which quite a respectable number of houses had been erected. I immediately made my way to the house of the police-master, to whom I had a letter of introduction, and was welcomed most cordially. Quarters were found for me in the fort, and I shall not easily forget the luxury of the wash and change of clothing which (especially the latter) I so much required.

My journey across the Kizil Kum desert was now finished, and no one could have been more satisfied than myself at its termination. Certainly, towards the end I began to have serious fears that I should not last it out; and when it is considered that the number of Europeans who have crossed that particular route can be counted on the fingers of one hand, the task is not to be belittled.

CHAPTER XXVI.

THE DESERT RIDE FINISHED

MY arrival at Petro-Alexandrovsk naturally filled me with a great satisfaction, even although in order to get to civilisation again several hundreds of miles of desert would have to be crossed. The satisfaction came about by reason of having accomplished the purpose which I had set myself to do. Khiva was now only a matter of sixty versts away, and this in an oasis overflowing with vegetation of all descriptions, and where roads of some sort would lead me briskly to my destination.

I had passed through a country, the Turgai, the Kizil Kum, and Kara Kum deserts, which I must, in spite of whatever discomforts I underwent, vote as being more interesting than any I had seen before; this, of course, mainly on account of the people, the nomadic, warlike, yet

gentle Khirghiz. I had passed through the fringe
of the Middle Horde and right through the centre
of the Little Horde, and in place of being subjected to that wretchedness and anxiety which
I had pictured, my progress, so far as the nomads
were concerned, was one of perfect safety.

I cannot make out why it is that the Khirghiz
have such a bad name in Russia. While in
Siberia some two years ago I had the opportunity of mixing freely with the Khirghiz of the
Great Horde, and was even then astonished at
the gentle character of the people, so glaring a
contrast was it to the word pictures painted by
Russians. Everything that was bad was attri-
buted to the Khirghiz. They were dirty, they
were cut-throats, they were thieves of the meanest
character, they were people whose words were
absolutely unreliable, and so on and so forth.
My Siberian experiences were the contrary, and
as a matter of fact I frequently placed myself
at their entire disposal when absolutely alone
and hundreds of miles from the nearest centre.
I found the Khirghiz of Siberia hospitable to a
fault. Indeed their character compared favour-

ably with that of the ordinary Russian. In travelling through the Turgai, however, I had been promised that with the Middle Horde I should find some of the most desperate characters in the dominions of the Czar. Military officers, whose education should surely have taught them better, told me that it was absolutely impossible to subjugate these wild people, who lived by preying upon each other, and whose keenest delight was in the cutting of throats. Journeying as I did through the Middle Horde practically alone, that is to say with only one attendant in the shape of the yemshik of a tarantass, I was in very little more protected state than when I journeyed through Siberia, and though my nights had frequently to be spent in the neighbourhood or the company of these wanderers of the steppe and desert, in place of being subjected to annoyance or being placed in jeopardy, I was received by the Khirghiz with every demonstration of welcome, and speedily found that my life was as safe or safer in their hands than might be the case with the somewhat mixed Slav people forming the population of Siberia.

R

I cannot trace in any books written on the district of the Turgai and the Kara Kum many intelligent references concerning these people. Their character, their religion, their manners, customs, and internal control are summed up in a few crisp, pointed sentences. We learn that they are treacherous, that they are lazy, and their existence of no possible benefit to the state. Reading between the lines one might well judge that in preferring a nomadic life the Khirghiz has placed individual comfort and predilection before any desires evinced on the part of the subjugator. Do what the Government of Russia will, it cannot induce the Khirghiz to abandon his tent life for that of the town dweller. It cannot induce him to throw up his somewhat unprofitable sheep and camel rearing for the probably more profitable commercial pursuits of towns. In the district of Semipalatinsk it is true that some Khirghiz have been wheedled over by Government officials to become labourers in the gold mines, but it is also true that the Khirghiz does not settle down long to this kind of labour. He is·in every sense of the term a Cossack, that is to say a horseman. He lives on his horse, he desires no better shelter, summer or winter, than that which is afforded by his kibitka. He loves not the vicinity of rivers or mountains; his paradise is the wide, boundless steppe. Whatever comforts there may be in the civilised life he does not crave for. A piece of half-raw mutton, a drink of koumiss, a drink of tea, and his cup of happiness is at the full. One would think that on these premises the Khirghiz is, after all, but little removed from the beast, since his desires are so unworldly. But the Khirghiz, on the contrary, is a most intelligent individual —intelligent, of course, when his environment is taken into consideration. The steppe has certainly given him a melancholy which is not observable amongst other semi-Mongolian races, such as the Tartars of Middle Russia, or the Buriats of Eastern Siberia. This melancholy is displayed in his music and his songs, which are always of the same sad order. The music, indeed, cannot be listened to without a feeling of melancholy creeping over one, and the words of the songs, when translated, have reference to subjects which are anything but joy-inspiring.

I discovered too that they were philosophers of the first water. This struck me particularly in crossing the desert. When an accident happened, or difficulties were in the way, they evinced a Mark Tapley cheerfulness, which was certainly not in keeping with the situation. Each time that difficulties arose in our way they were ever ready with some quotation or other bearing upon that particular subject. Thus on the breakdown of my telega once by the smashing of a wheel, Osman, first in the Khirghiz and then in the Russian languages, said, " The sun is round, the moon is round, the stars are round. Who has made them ? He who has made them will make us another wheel, and that will be round also."

At Kazalinsk I had the good fortune to meet a gentleman well learned in the Khirghiz dialects, and, during my long journey from Orenburg, I had phonetically taken down several Khirghiz expressions, which became familiar after much repetition. I was astonished to discover the subtlety of the Khirghiz, and the wide range of intelligence which seemed to pervade the humblest of the tribe. I found, for instance, that the following expression, which became familiar to me at every meeting and parting with a Khirghiz, was known throughout the length and breadth of Turkestan, so that even children would repeat it glibly.

"When thou goest in the company of a good man you will come up to the mark; when thou goest in the company of a bad man you will be ashamed."

Amongst other interesting proverbs which I managed to secure *en route* and get translated at Petro-Alexandrovsk are the following. Their philosophy will speak for itself.

1. "The satisfied man is not a good companion for the hungry!"

2. "He who drinks stolen milk openly is safe, but he who licks the pail surreptitiously is caught."

3. "When the Sart (Khivans or Bokharans) is happing rich he builds a house; when the Khirghiz is happing rich he acquires one more wife."

4. "When the raven kisses his young one he says, 'My beautiful white'; when the hedgehog kisses his young one he says, 'My most soft.'"

5. "The steppe is not without a wolf; the nation is not without a thief."

6. "What is pleasing to the people is not pleasing to the king; what is pleasing to the king is not pleasing to the people."

7. "When someone comes to drink at the stream, then is not the time to cloud the water."

One thing which struck me as peculiar was the extreme dignity with which the Khirghiz held themselves when in contact with either Sarts, Khivans, Bokharans, Uzbecs, or Tartars. It is safe to assume that the Sarts, as town dwellers, were, taking it altogether, more intelligent and probably more industrious and of good to the community at large than the Khirghiz, but the latter treated the town dwellers with a lofty contempt, a contempt which was at times amusing. Indeed the Khivans whom we met *en route* were subjected in several small ways to indignities on the part of the Khirghiz, which it seemed to me to be rather unnecessary, but I learned that the Khivans preferred a wholesome respect for the denizens of the desert, and it must be admitted that a man or a tribe who will or which will prefer an existence such as that which the Khirghiz loves must be a man or a people out of the ordinary.

Another feature is their common poverty. The head-man of a tribe lives in very little better style than the humblest member. His kibitka is, perhaps, a little better decorated, but his food and his koumiss are the same. He is in his daily life but a simple horseman, and shares with the lowliest of the particular section the common misfortunes or fortunes. The spirit of socialism seems to rank here higher than in any other community of the world. With no rent to pay, no land to till, with all their desires acceded to by nature in the shape of rapidly breeding sheep and cattle, there is but little difference between the head-man of a Khirghiz section and the humblest member. Each has his horse or horses, each has his wife or wives, each eats mutton, drinks koumiss and tea. The raiment of each is practically the same. Nothing more can be had, for nothing more does the desert give. Opportunities there are of the Khirghiz becoming rich if they will only set cunning to work and enter the field of competition known to the Russians, but the Khirghiz sees in those crowded towns and in the hurry and bustle of business a something which appals him. He prefers the liberty of the desert to the so-called comforts of civilisation. His greatest dread is that the Czar in his might should call upon him to abandon his mode of life, or institute such measures that the freedom of that life should be cramped or in some way interfered with.

CHAPTER XXVII.

PETRO-ALEXANDROVSK

I WAS received in the fort of Petro-Alexandrovsk by M. Galkin, a gentleman of culture, who acts as administrator of the Khivan province so far as Russian interests are concerned. Monsieur Galkin spoke a little English. He is one of those who acted for the Russian Government in the delimitation of the Pamirs some years ago, and it was while undertaking this work that he fell in with many English officers and so acquired some knowledge of our language. He received me very hospitably, and gave me every facility for getting to Khiva.

I elected, however, to remain in Petro-Alexandrovsk for three days, as I was still far from well, and utterly wearied of the whole thing. Furthermore, I was told that it would be better for me to remain in the fort until I received the special permission of the Khan to cross the Oxus river and enter Khivan territory proper. Monsieur Galkin sent his dragoman to Khiva on this mission, begging at the same time the privilege of a Khivan escort and accommodation for me on reaching the city.

I was very astonished to find in Petro-Alexandrovsk a community of Russians and a town of some proportions. On the outskirts of Petro-Alexandrovsk there were some few Khivan, Uzbec, and Sart dwellings, but around the military laager there had grown up during the occupation of the Russians quite a respectable colony, in which the Russian style of architecture had ousted in some measure the extraordinary style of erections used by the Asiatics. Considering that Petro-Alexandrovsk is completely out of communication with the outside world, desert being on every hand, it was astonishing to be received by Russian functionaries, who, it struck me, were above the average in intelligence and sociability. I was accorded quarters in the house of a Russian engineer, a house possessing one of the most beautiful gardens I have ever seen. The police-master and the inspector of the lazaret hospital vied with each other to promote my comfort, so that under the advice of the doctor I was speedily restored to my usual health.

Since Fort Petro-Alexandrovsk was founded by General von Kaufmann its military aspect has diminished considerably, and instead of being at the present time simply a fort, it is in some respects quite a small commercial town. The Russians, ever good traders, have seized the opportunity of using Petro-Alexandrovsk as a sort of barter place, where the Khivan workers in metals, silks, and stuffs can come and trade their productions for Russian utensils or for money. This has meant the springing into being of a large number of shops and magazines in the big square by the church. In fact, it was very extraordinary to see in this little oasis on the banks of the Oxus river a town Russian in every particular, possessing the usual Greek orthodox church of an architecture essentially Russian, and with houses surrounding it built, not óf mud or sand and clay, but wood. The Russian, it seems, is nothing if not Russian, and here in a part of the world where wood is of extreme value, the Russian preferred to spend a large amount of money in order to erect a log house rather than take advantage of the more natural building material, clay and sand, such as had been used by the Khivans and Sarts from the time Khiva was first built.

This national idiosyncrasy is to be found everywhere, and it exists from one end of the empire to the other. In Siberia and Russia, the national Muscovite costume for the male consists of top-boots, baggy trousers, a red shirt with a belt around it, and a white peaked cap. This costume adorns nearly every male Russian from Warsaw to Vladivostock, and here in Petro-Alexandrovsk, where it was distinctly out of place owing to the great heat of summer, it was still used by the Muscovite population of the lower order. With the merchants and the functionaries the all-prevailing white jacket, brass buttons, white hat and high boots were always to be found; and what a contrast it was, this decidedly uncomfortable style of costume, when compared to that of the native Khivan, whose dress is certainly more in

conformity with the climate. Sandals, a long and
thick gown fastened around the centre by a multi-
coloured scarf, a white or green turban, or the
thick sheepskin bonnet.

I was delighted to find that in Petro-Alexandrovsk quite a large number of Russian comestibles were obtainable, and my eyes bulged when,
on turning over the stock of the biggest dealer
there one day, I discovered half a dozen tins of
canned lobster. How long they had been there
I do not venture to suggest. The Russian proprietor did not offer any explanation. I only
know that the cans looked very, very old, but
I bought the lot on the spot, glad to get anything
which was out of the common.

The doctor of the lazaret told me that Petro-
Alexandrovsk owed its present existence to the
number of soldiers, on their military service being
completed, electing to remain in the fort rather
than go back to Russia. At the present time
there are only two companies of infantry and one
battery of artillery in the fort. When the conquest of Khiva was completed, a large force was
maintained for some years afterwards in order to

overawe the then warlike population in the Khivan oasis, and small forays had continually to be made to punish certain rebellious subjects of the Khan. For at least fifteen years, however, the Khivans have been nothing if not peaceable. It is true that amongst themselves there are a great many things done which, looked at from the point of view of civilisation, spell barbarism with a very big B. Robbery and murder are of frequent occurrence in the smaller towns of the Khanate. Justice as meted out by the Khan and his ministers is of a very scrappy and unreliable character, but the Khivans to a man have come to recognise the fact that they have only to let the Russians alone and they themselves will not be interfered with.

It seemed to me, indeed, that the Russians at Petro-Alexandrovsk are simply there watching and waiting for the time when, by their own barbaric methods, the Khivan population shall dwindle and ultimately die out.

The climate of the oasis, said the doctor, was by no means bad. In Petro-Alexandrovsk itself, where a system of drainage had been instituted

THE GATE OF KHIVA, FROM WITHIN

A KHIVAN RECEPTION

and swamps obliterated, the percentage of mortality was not greater than in ordinary Siberian towns, but in Khiva and in the other Khivan towns and villages it was frightful, owing principally to the absolute lack of sanitation, and the retention of enormous tracts of morass, which bred malaria of the most pronounced type. Khiva and the Khivan province, with the splendid waterway of the Oxus flowing through it, could be made into a veritable paradise, but with the Asiatic in power there, and without there being any reason for its retention as a city or as a province, it was not to the interests of Russia to promote its development. On the other hand, the finest thing that can happen for Russia, so far as Khiva is concerned, is that it shall ultimately become obliterated. It is of no earthly use to the Government. It necessitates the establishment of a governor of the province, with administrator and a whole host of functionaries. Its products are dwindling in importance, its power is feeble, and, taken altogether, it is more of a nuisance than anything else to the Russian Government.

I have already spoken of the admirable irrigation system in use. I heard that this irrigation had been instituted many hundreds, perhaps thousands, of years ago, probably soon after the time when the Oxus changed its course and flowed to the north to empty itself in the Aral Sea. It is abundantly clear that at one time or another the district of Khiva must have been desert, for all the way up the Oxus to Charjui the sands come right to the bank of the river, except here and there where natives have formed little colonies, and by digging canals and raising the water have converted unprofitable sandy stretches into luxurious and beautiful gardens. This irrigating system has been further improved by the Russians, so that every inch of land saved from the desert is under active cultivation. Crops grow with extreme rapidity, fruit of every description ripens to perfection. Such semi-tropical fruit as figs, melons, and pomegranates attain enormous proportions in a very few weeks. Grapes are literally a glut, they grow everywhere; in fact, the whole of the oasis of Petro-Alexandrovsk forms an enormous fruit and vegetable garden.

On the third day of my stay the dragoman

of the Khan arrived, and Monsieur Galkin in addition gave me the assistance of his own dragoman, a Khirghiz who spoke the Russian and Sart languages. The two dragomans travelled in a small drosky kept by a local horse dealer, and I rode my bicycle. It was not far to the banks of the Oxus, and here we had to cross the wide stream by means of flat-bottomed boats pulled by towers. The Oxus at this point forms a perfect delta, little islands arising all over the place, the whole width being, perhaps, two miles. It was a long and wearisome job getting across the river, more especially as it was necessary to tow a long way against the stream before a fordable place could be reached, so that the towers could drag us across. It took us five hours to reach the opposite bank, and here a swamp obstructed progress for a considerable time. At length, however, some sort of a made road was reached, a narrow lane-like thoroughfare between high mud walls. The dust was calf deep, a white alkali-like dust, which caused the eyes to smart and the lips to crack. Generally this little lane ran by the side of an irrigating

S

ditch, and I saw several of the peculiar engines by which the Khivans raise water from one ditch to the other. These engines take the form of a huge wheel, on which are fastened a large number of earthenware bottles slanting diagonally. The wheel is revolved by means of a wooden cog laid horizontally, the motive power being a camel, which walks in a circle, its eyes being tightly bandaged to prevent it going giddy. The water raised by each bottle falls, as it turns over, into a wooden trough, which carries it to the higher ditch.

The walls of the irrigating ditches are composed of a light grey clay, and the water itself, owing to the large amount of mud and sediment, is thick and gluey. Yet this water is used as it is, even by the Khan himself. It is Oxus water, brought straight from the river by means of small canals and ditches, raised one above the other; Khiva, as a matter of fact, standing some feet above the level of the river.

We passed through the Khivan town of Khanki, where we received the hospitality of the beg or head - man. Essentially Oriental was Khanki, indescribably filthy, reminding me strongly of some places I have seen in Asia Minor, except that the architecture of the little town was more Egyptian than Turkish. The houses are all built on the slanting Egyptian style, the bases of the walls being sometimes five or six feet thick, and the top tapering to a few inches. The insides of the walls are perfectly perpendicular, but the exterior walls, on all sides, have a pronounced slant. Buttresses are used at every corner in order to give stability to the fabric. In the construction of the houses no straw is used, and the main supports consist of a few trees joined at each corner. I saw a house in course of erection. Poles about thirty feet high are planted at each corner, and the wall is built up between these from clay. There is no system of framework whatever. The walls are built soft, and the consequence is that before the top is reached the wall assumes all sorts of fantastic shapes, while as soon as the hot sun has thoroughly baked the clay huge cracks appear on every hand. Windows are almost unknown, and the Khivans appear to have no idea how to make them. For instance, in Khanki nearly all the houses have a platform of clay erected in front of the house, over which a canopy of boughs is built. The entrance to the house is effected through an irregular opening in the mud wall, sometimes twenty feet high, possessing no door. It is on the platform in front of his house that the Khivan practically lives. His cooking arrangements are open to the public gaze, he performs his ablutions, such as they are, here; in fact, the necessity of a house at all seemed to me to be very questionable, since in summer the Khivan lives, eats, and sleeps on the clay platform in the open.

The interior of these houses is gloomy enough, the flooring generally of clay, with bits of Bokharan or Khivan carpet thrown loosely about. A sleeping apartment is as bare as a cell, for the Khivan abjures cushions or pillows, being content to curl himself up on a mat and so seek repose. There is absolutely no attempt whatever at sanitation. Sewage is thrown directly into the middle of the street, and here a mass of putrefying animal and vegetable garbage causes the air to fairly reek. Yet in Khanki fruit flows as from a cornucopia. Grapes, melons, pomegranates, and figs were placed before me. Tea was made from the ditch water, but it was so horribly thick and dirty that I preferred not to drink it, and regretted extremely that I had not brought a tub of water with me from the fort.

From here our way led us through dust-choked lanes and past innumerable irrigating canals and ditches. We encountered now and again parties of Khivans engaged in agricultural pursuits, or, mounted on camels, making their way from one point to another.

CHAPTER XXVIII.

THE GATES OF KHIVA

I WAS not destined to enter the city without an adventure. The Khivans, it should be mentioned, use a somewhat extraordinary vehicle, which they call by the general Mohammedan term "araba." The Khivan araba is a two-wheeled affair, the wheels of which are ten feet, twelve feet, and sometimes fifteen feet high. These ungainly and seemingly unnecessarily high wheels facilitate the passage through sandy stretches and morasses. The body of the vehicle is placed on the axle, and generally consists of a big platform upon which it would be no difficult matter for twenty men to find sitting room.

It was when almost within sight of the walls of Khiva that such an araba drawn by a couple of camels came trundling our way. The platform of the vehicle was crowded with Khivans, who, upon seeing me, yelled with laughter, for, although I had taken the precaution to adopt a semi-

Oriental costume, it was easy for them to perceive that I was a white man. The emissary of the Khan who accompanied me was furious at their raillery, and instantly ordered his two jigitas to turn back and punish the occupants of the araba for their insolence. No sooner said than done. The two horsemen turned and made for the araba like the wind. Reaching it, one by one they dragged the men from the vehicle, lashing at them all the time with their long whips, the wretched fellows doing nothing to protect themselves, but instead burying their faces in the ground praying for mercy. The dragoman ordered more and more punishment, the long whip-thongs hissed and cracked down upon the squirming crowd. Kicks were freely dealt out by the committee of punishment, blood began to run, and piteous cries rose upon the air. It was a sight to see the unfortunate Khivans thus sprawling in the dust, and I stood an amazed spectator of this extraordinary scene. Now and again some Khivan would endeavour to seize the boot of one of his assailants in order to kiss it and so obtain pardon. As for the two dragomans, the Khivan stood up in the drosky directing the ceremony, while the Khirghiz lay back on his pillow and fairly howled with laughter.

"Let them be thankful," said the Khirghiz dragoman to me, "that they get nothing more. It is quite within the power of the Khan's drago-man to take them into Khiva, where they would all be thrown into prison, if not flogged far worse than they have been."

My heart gave a great jump when, rounding a bend in the narrow road, I saw, a few hundred yards off, a crumbling battlemented wall, and a little further off a high gateway.   It was the wall, it was the gate of Khiva!   The horses of the drosky and of the jigitas threw up great clouds of white dust.   I was smothered from head to foot, and my face was caked, but there ahead was Khiva.   Larger and larger became the walls, and soon we passed through the crumbling gateway.

What a sight met my eyes when I dismounted to gaze upon this famous city!   Ruin and dis-order spread in every direction.   The great walls, seventy to eighty feet high and proportionately thick, were broken, and lay in great heaps of sun-baked clay on all hands.   Huge gaps appeared here and there.   The roadway which we had to traverse was simply a chaos of dismantled wall. The scene was impressive—here was Khiva, but what a Khiva! I saw irregular lanes bordered by tall, gloomy walls, all in an extreme state of decay, stretching here and there. Filthy ditches ran down the centre of these lanes; shadow and gloom was everywhere. The atmosphere was white with dust and reeked horribly. Down these narrow lane-like streets we picked our way cautiously, stumbling in the gloom against crouching Khivans, or kicking out of the way sore and miserable dogs that prowled everywhere. At the corners beggars, blind, maimed, or covered with horrible sores, sat in small clusters, with hands outstretched, and, hearing the jangle of the drosky bells, howled for alms.

We passed on and presently entered a broader thoroughfare, where was a bazaar roofed over with boughs and branches of trees, but where filth, as in all other parts, reigned supreme. Khivans began to crowd around us, but the jigitas rode forward and used their whips mercilessly upon the populace. There was some laughter and shouting as I went through. Staid Moslems, seated on their little platforms in front of their shops, tumbled into the procession. Then out of the bazaar we went until we brought up at a high wall, through which a narrow entrance led to what looked like the bowels of the earth. Down this alley we went, stumbling our way over the broken ground and feeling our way through the pitchy darkness. The rabble remained at the entrance, for this was, let it be known, the residence of Mohamed Mat Murat, Prime Minister of the Khan and the richest man in Khiva.

We debouched into a little courtyard, the dragomans descended and motioned me to follow them. Through narrow passages, so low built that we had to stoop, we went, until a mat was pushed aside and I entered the courtyard of the "palace."

I had arrived. That last day's journey of sixty versts, although not of course so harassing or wearying as some days on the desert, was sufficiently fatiguing to make me glad that the whole thing was over. Gratified as I was at having completed my cycle ride to Khiva, I yet felt a strange, unaccountable desire to get out of it as speedily as possible. The gloom, the wretchedness, the utter decay on every hand filled me with anything but inspiring feelings. My first glimpse of Khiva had brought to me a great shock. I had read Burnaby and several other writers who have visited the city in previous years, but my first glimpse convinced me of one .thing, that I saw Khiva in a far different state to that in which it presented itself to them. The suggestion of the doctor in Petro-Alexandrovsk that the Russians were simply waiting for Khiva to die out had here ample corroboration, and, during the three days I remained in the city, it became patent to me that Khiva is absolutely doomed to obliteration within a few short years.

The palace of the Prime Minister of Khiva was a mud-built erection containing a large number of dark and fearsome passages, small cell-like rooms, scarcely one of which contained a single article of furniture. The room apportioned to my use was about fifteen feet square, floor, walls, and ceiling composed of clay. There was no furniture, with the exception of one small table and a rough wooden settee. Carpets were thrown promiscuously in various corners ; there was no ornamentation of any sort. The doorway was covered by a gaudy mat, there was a window about two feet square admitting a dim light from the gloomy courtyard without. This courtyard was tolerably large, in the centre of which was a pond, the edges green and slimy from accumulated vegetation. I looked upon this pond with some degree of suspicion, because I had an idea that it was responsible for much of the stink which hung about the place. Imagine my astonishment, then, when I evinced a desire to remove some of the dirt I had accumulated on the journey, to be invited to the edge of this pond and perform my ablutions therein. It was a case of doing as Khivans did, so I washed in that way, found that such a thing as a towel was unknown in Khiva, and wiped myself on a pocket-handkerchief. Nor was my surprise at this novel way of doing things lessened when the little Khivan boy who had been told off to prepare some hot water for tea, came and filled his copper vessel at the pond.

Having thus cleaned myself I was told that food awaited me. The Khirghiz dragoman and myself therefore sat down in my little apartment cross-legged and tackled " pilau," a dish composed

of mutton and rice, in every respect similar to
that of Turkey. Bread there was none, but a
flat slab of dough, something like a pancake, took
its place. It was difficult indeed for me to eat the
"pilau," but I made up for edibles in an attack
upon nearly a hundredweight of fruit which had
been brought in.

Then came a message from the Prime Minister
that he would be pleased to see me. Accompanied by the dragoman I crossed the courtyard
and entered the apartments of Mat Murat.
Solemn and gloomy they were. Here and there
we nearly fell headlong over some Khivan crouched
in passages or at corners, a little boy carrying
a small lamp dangling from a chain preceding us.
A curtain was thrown aside, and Mohamed Mat
Murat was revealed to me. He was a somewhat
tall, grave, and extremely old man; his long, white
beard hung on his breast, his copper-coloured face
was wrinkled and gnarled. He sat on the floor,
cross-legged, and held out both his hands to me
in token of welcome. Then he motioned to me
to sit beside him, and entered into a long series
of questions, which I answered as best I could.
I found him a rather intelligent old man, although

it was a very difficult matter for me to converse with him, more especially as the Khirghiz dragoman I had with me spoke execrable Russian, worse perhaps than I did. The Prime Minister evinced a great desire to know something about my own country. He perfectly well remembered the visit of Dr. Lansdell to Khiva, but when questioned on Colonel Burnaby he could not remember. He reckoned, however, that I was the fourth European, with the exception of Russians, who had visited Khiva and had been entertained by him.

I pointed out that this must surely be a mistake, as some ten Europeans had, for various purposes, visited Khiva. He remembered Edward Moser, the Hungarian, but had no knowledge whatever of Vambery, nor could he remember Richard McGahan, the American journalist, the account of whose plucky ride during the days of the fall of Khiva was so well and so widely circulated. The difficulties of our conversation elicited a surprising fact. It was this, that within twelve versts of Khiva there existed a small colony peopled entirely by Germans. I scarcely believed my ears that here in the middle of a barbaric country there

should be a Teutonic colony. But the explanation
was soon forthcoming. It was explained that at
the time when General von Kaufmann marched
across the desert from Orenburg he had with
him a large number of German camp-followers,
and, being German himself, he put them under
his especial protection. When Khiva fell, and the
various other expeditions were organised against
southern and eastern Turkestan, these camp-
followers still remained in Kaufmann's train, and
Skobeleff, who was general of the Turkestan
forces, subsequently got leave of the Khan of
Bokhara to allow the Germans to remain in the
vicinity of Bokhara. They formed a little colony
and gradually multiplied, but some fifteen years
ago a secession took place, and about forty men
and women accepted the invitation of the Khan
of Khiva and travelled over the desert to the
banks of the Oxus. The Khan received them
kindly, and forthwith gave them a large tract of
land near the city and employed them in various
ways. As a matter of fact, these Germans are
the only artificers of any good in the vicinity of
Khiva. They were the first to make glass and

window-panes, and constructed chairs and tables and carriages of some reasonable shape and form.

I was so delighted at the knowledge that I begged the Prime Minister to send a man to the colony in order to get a German who would act as interpreter, and begged permission also to visit the colony, permission which was at once granted me. I was also told that the son of the Khan, and future ruler of Khiva, had signified his desire to see me the following day, when I should also have the privilege of an audience with the Khan. Anxious, therefore, to get a proper interpreter, I got my dragoman to send someone to the German colony at once, and that same evening there arrived one Emile Reeson, head-man of the German colony. He wore Khivan costume, came in and salaamed in the peculiar Oriental fashion. Then he waited until everyone had cleared from the room, threw off his long silk waist-scarf, threw off his long gown, removed his Khivan shako, and I saw he had on a frock coat, a pair of trousers, a pair of boots, and—strangest fact of all—a collar and tie, something which I had not seen for months.

I lay back and gasped.

MAT-MURAT, PRIME MINISTER AND TREASURER TO THE KHAN

CHAPTER XXIX.

KHIVA THE DECAYING

AFTER one day within the precincts of Khiva I was by no means anxious to prolong my stay. All the accounts, graphic and otherwise, that I had read of this celebrated city appeared far too coloured when with the naked eye I surveyed this scene of squalor and wretchedness. Khiva, the half-way stage between Turkestan and Europe, the city of the Khans, the stronghold of the Sart races, now but a mass of crumbling ruins; a huddled population which seems to the European eye to be simply awaiting the end. There is a sadness about the place which is overwhelming. There is nothing inspiriting, nothing to afford to the ear or the eye the slightest recompense for labour spent. Khiva is a sore in more senses than one, it is a stench which the wholesome desert surrounding it could do

T
273

well without. When, years ago, great caravans trailed from the Afghan and Chinese borders *en route* to Europe, and paused for rest and revelry at Khiva, this city may have been a great place, where Eastern hospitality and Eastern magnificence were to be seen at their height. Now, when no caravans pass that way, when through the aggressive enterprise of the Russian two iron rails have been laid by "the edge of the world" on the Afghan frontier, and a fleet of steamers has been put on the Caspian sea, and the grim heights of the Caucasus have been encompassed by other railway lines, the days of the caravan are past and Khiva is lost, given over to the desert to dwindle and die.

At the time of the conquest Khiva, as a province, was passing rich, and it is a commentary that at the present time the Khan still lives, and Mat Murat, Prime Minister, still lives, and for twenty-five or twenty-six years have been enabled to watch the decline of their country. Narrower and narrower becomes the zone of influence of the Khan of Khiva. Slowly but surely the marauding Turcomans creep towards it from the west, less and less becomes the sphere of influence of Khiva to the east and the south, so that the 35,700 square miles of territory subdued by General von Kaufmann is but an ambitious mileage to give present Khivan influence. The war indemnity, fixed at what under present circumstances must be conceded an absurd figure, is mainly the cause of Khiva's decay. In 1874 it was possible for the 110,000 inhabitants of Khiva to meet this indemnity with but little effort. With a dwindling population and a great diminution of income from outside sources, the whole province is plunged in despair, not so much on account of the future of the province, but by reason of the steady refusals of the Russian authorities to take over the Khanate and administer it by Russian methods.

There stands on the banks of the Oxus a fort menacing Khiva ; there stands on the other bank a decrepit monarchy, a population dwindling year by year, without hope, without the slightest desire of ever becoming anything greater. Khiva, as a province, is eaten up by the war indemnity. It has been reduced to abject poverty by this war indemnity. The merciless Russian shows not the slightest desire to mitigate the sufferings of these people. Trade, commerce, intercommunication have been wrecked by the Russians. The strategical trans-Caspian railroad, tapping the rich centres of Central Asia, reduced at one blow the possibility of Khiva ever paying its debt. Thus Russia stands by waiting for Khiva to die, giving it the pill which will ensure a speedy demise in the shape of a war indemnity which can never be paid. The present style of government is undoubtedly the very best for Russia. The population of Khiva at the present time is about eighty thousand souls, a big diminution from 1880, when it numbered about one hundred and ten thousand. Eighty thousand people, with a considerable tract of land under cultivation and several important towns, would entail upon the administration of Russia an expenditure by no means commensurate with the advantages to be obtained. The treaty between Khiva and Russia left the Khan free to administer his own province. The Khan has undoubtedly repented his bargain. He sees himself a king

A KHIVAN STREET

THE FAMOUS TOWER OF KHIVA

amongst a dissatisfied people, a king in name
only, since he can do nothing except amongst
his own handful of people without the authority
of the Czar. Although densely ignorant, the
Khan has some idea of the fitness of things. I
heard that he described himself once as a prisoner
of Russia in a cell, but the cell, instead of having
walls composed of mud, was fitted with satin.
He, like his subjects, has settled to his fate. His
son, the future Khan, is probably more ambitious.
He it is who has had the greatest hand in the
present cultivation of the oasis, a cultivation which
threatened to decay some years ago. Upon the
death of the Khan the enthusiasm of the son for
the future is to be questioned. That annual
tribute of so many pieces in gold and silver is
bound to shake his faith. The wretchedness of
his people, his own personal wretchedness as a
matter of fact, will surely outweigh all his kingly
ideals.

Under the intelligent guidance of Emile Reeson
I made a tour of Khiva. I visited the several
mosques of the place, wretched edifices where
decay was evident on every hand, and saw some

of the workshops of the natives, where the celebrated Khivan silk carpets are manufactured. Primitiveness in these latter departments was the only thing I found of interest to me. Everything was done by hand; there was not the slightest idea of machinery. Even the handloom in existence some hundreds of years ago was not to be found in Khiva. In the blacksmiths' shops, where pots and pans were made, copper was the material most generally used. There was some idea of tinning, but all the work, fashioning and so forth, was accomplished entirely by the use of the hammer. I remarked on the plenitude of copper, since it seemed everything was made of this expensive metal. Whips which were used by the Khirghiz and Khivans, selling at only a few kopecks each, had their mountings made of copper. I learned, however, that on the north of Khiva, near the Aral Sea, the natives found copper in abundance. So plentiful is the metal that the Khivans tin all their utensils. I bought several native articles, which I thought at first were tin or zinc, but discovered they were real copper vessels tinned over.

Silk is manufactured in the most primitive manner possible, and one wonders, after viewing the method of manufacture, that such symmetry can be obtained in the completed article. Carpets are made entirely by hand; these carpets being mere strips, the fashion as varying as it is original.

Naturally, in such a fertile region, the chief production consists of fruit and vegetables. As it is impossible to export any of these productions and fully fifty per cent. goes to decay every year, the population appears to live mainly upon fruit and rice. What meat there is is obtainable only by the few merchants and officials, unless amongst the peasantry sheep - rearing is also resorted to as a means of livelihood. Amongst fruits the mulberry, apple, pear, cherry, plum, date, melon, peach, pomegranate, and grape are in great abundance. Wheat, rice, and barley are the principal cereals. Linseed, cotton and hemp are but little cultivated. Pumpkins, cucumbers, carrots, turnips, potatoes, cabbage, and such-like vegetables are given very small attention ; indeed, their cultivation does not seem to be well understood. One remarks at the jungle-like character of most of the gardens. Weeds grow to great lengths, and no effort seems to be directed towards their extermination. The reproductive character of the earth is such, however, that everything grows with great fecundity, so that the Khivan is but little troubled with the economic principles of agriculture or farming.

The city of Khiva itself is surrounded by two mud walls, both walls, however, being at the present time mere masses of ruins. The outside wall is about twelve feet high, and the inner wall a little higher. Near the gates, of which, in the outer wall, there are twelve, the mud embattlements are raised to a considerable height. The inner wall at the present time scarcely exists, the encroachments of the natives in the manufacture of mud dwellings having practically obliterated it. The streets themselves, as I have already said, are nothing more nor less than lanes, where the *débris* of old houses and the walls of Khiva lie everywhere higgledy-piggledy. The atmosphere is terrible. Throughout the whole of the day the sun is almost obscured by the thick white dust rising from the dried mud. Wind there seems to be none, so that the fetid stenches to be met with in every direction hang suspended in the air. The bazaar, the only scene of activity in the whole city, is a poor, miserable place. Little of a purchasable character is displayed for sale. Fruit seems to be the only article in any quantity; the manufactured articles are but rarely seen. What becomes of the copper utensils, the silk stuffs and carpets is a mystery. Caravans now rarely start from Khiva, no one passes through *en route* to the north or to the south. The bazaar, which, as in other eastern lands, is the only centre, here in Khiva tells the tale of that city's decrepitude emphatically.

That day I saw the son of the Khan. We had wandered through evil-smelling streets until I became fairly smothered in dust and disreputable to look at. We had rounded a corner, passed through a small alley, debouched into a courtyard, when Emile Reeson tugged my elbow, and the next moment I was bowing to the son of the Khan. He motioned me to sit down beside him. He was a tall, sallow young man, with big melancholy eyes. He gave the salaam in the Oriental

fashion, and made inquiries with regard to the
health of my wives, my children, my sheep, oxen,
and my camels. I did not even suggest that I
possessed no cattle and no more wives than one,
since such a confession might have led to difficulties best avoided. The Khan's son, it appeared,
had received intelligence from some outside
sources of a great war then being carried on
between the English-speaking people and Spain,
and wanted to know how it was progressing.
Had I known the slough opened at my feet I
would never have endeavoured to explain the
difference between America and England, and the
cause of the war between Spain and the United
States. It was question and answer on this one
subject throughout the whole of an hour, when,
sunset coming, certain ministers and others came
into the courtyard, went down on their hands and
knees and- knocked their heads on the mud
flooring. Emile Reeson gave me the signal, the
Khan's son salaamed, and the interview was over.

Passing through the darkening and deserted
streets we came to an open doorway from which
weird music emanated, a sound of drums and

cymbals banging and clanging. I paused listen-
ing, and a Khivan coming out of the entrance
saw me. An animated conversation then arose
between my German interpreter and the Khivan,
and I was asked to go inside. A strange scene
met my gaze. In a small, square apartment,
reeking with vile smoke, sat cross-legged some
fifty or more Khivans, all with their huge bonnets
on. In the centre was a square of carpet, whereon
knelt a small boy. I thought at first it was a girl,
because the costume was long and the hair hung
right to the waist. In one corner sat an orchestra.
There were drums made of gourds covered with
sheepskin, cymbals of copper, and one or two reed
instruments, the whole combining to set up a din
which was deafening. The child on the carpet
kept twisting its thumbs and fingers, snapping
them occasionally and wriggling its shoulders,
stomach, and body in unison to the bellowing of
the band. His eyes rolled, and he kept shaking
his head spasmodically. The Khivans around
looked on with eyes of intense admiration.
Suddenly the boy stood up, howled out something, and instantly the carpet was snatched away.

Then the boy began to dance, a slow, rhythmic dance at first, changing then to a whirl, spinning round and round like a top. I had seen in Scutari the whirling dervishes—this boy was simply whirling as did the dervishes. His arms were outstretched, his head was thrown back, his long black hair and his dress floated out in circles. Round and round he spun, faster and faster at every revolution, meanwhile that the band in the corner laboured at their work like Trojans. The reed pipes screeched, the cymbals clashed with increasing fury, the drums rattled and bumped and thumped until I felt that I was being deafened. Hoarse cries resounded through the room ; men on their haunches wriggled and waved their hands in apparent ecstasy. Then of a sudden the dancer fell limp and inert, bathed in perspiration. Willing hands raised him up, and wooden bowls containing seloni tea, or a decoction made from half-matured tea, were forced upon him. The band ceased, only the guttural chatter of the natives was now to be heard, but the sweat poured in streams, and I rose and hurried with all my might from the spot.

CHAPTER XXX.

MY RECEPTION BY THE KHAN

M Y interview with the Khan of Khiva was short and unprofitable. I must confess that I had no particular desire to see the Khan at all. But it seemed to be the established custom of everyone visiting Khiva that a visit should be paid to his Highness. I was fearful at first for my appearance. My clothes were in a sad condition, and, knowing what Oriental potentates are, I was rather anxious than otherwise to get out of the ordeal. Emile Reeson, however, suggested that if I left without seeing the Khan, his Highness would be offended, and he offered to rig me out in Khivan costume in order to pay the visit, suggesting that my adopting the Khivan costume would be a compliment to the Khan. This was done. The remnants of my own Oriental costume were used in conjunction with several other things which Reeson procured for me, so that I presented, I think, a fairly passable appearance, although my greatest difficulty was to use my hands. The long costume of the Khivan possesses sleeves nearly double the ordinary length. They are very much like the Chinese sleeves, and have always to be kept up by the bend of the arm. Immediately the arm is straightened the length of sleeve falls down so that they can easily drag in the dust. I was continually tripping over my gown too, and the weight of it, for it seemed to be composed of two layers of silk over a layer of thick wool, made me bend. My headpiece consisted of a small round skull-cap, composed of various coloured wares and tinsel ornaments.

Thus arrayed I took my seat in the small drosky, and after parading before the eyes of Khiva's multitudes, presented myself before the Khan. Whatever surprise he may have conceived at my appearance he certainly betrayed none. He took my hands in solemn fashion, jerked them upwards once, twice, then dropped them. He waved his hand and motioned to me to sit beside

him. We were in the courtyard. Before us was
a little stagnant pool of water, similar to that in
the palace of Mat Murat. Behind us, a low, mean
building of mud, was the palace of the Khan.
Emile Reeson at once opened the conversation.
There were the usual inquiries regarding my
health, whether I had plenty to eat, and how
my wives, children, and cattle were. These were
all diplomatically answered, and I then sought
the opportunity of asking the Khan about my
English predecessors in Khiva. He did not seem
to be very pleased with the questions, and shook
his head as Reeson propounded them. He could
not think, he could not remember, he said. Yes,
he did remember a doctor some years ago.

Then, like his son, he began to question me
on the Spanish-American war. Strange that
the topic of conversation amongst the rulers of
Khiva should be a campaign between these
countries. I went through the formula of the
day previous, but the Khan, whether Reeson
did not explain sufficiently lucidly, or whether he
was bored with the interview, did not evince
much interest. He again asked me whether I

had enough to eat, and whether my quarters were comfortable, and then held out his hands as a signal that the interview was concluded.

I learned, however, on my arrival at the palace of Mat Murat that in response to my request the Khan had graciously presented me with a signed portrait of himself, nearly the last one remaining of a collection, and had given instructions that I should be plentifully supplied with fruit during my stay.

That same afternoon I decided to visit the German colony, but my German interpreter, for some strange reason, desired me to come a little later in the day. He would like to go forward first, and suggested that my Khirghiz dragoman could drive me over. This request seemed to me reasonable, for I half suspected that Reeson wanted to get on ahead to inform his compatriots of my proposed visit. It was a troublesome twelve versts, for the way ran over a rank marshland. I was informed that the water here was absolutely deadly. It was many years old, but so clear that in some of the pools one could see through it as through glass, but this water was far worse than the germ-infested flowing waters of the irrigating ditches. This information was elicited by the efforts put forward by our yemshik to prevent the natural impulse of the horses to drink.

The country, although grass-grown, and with here and there rich pasture-lands and fruit gardens, presented a miserable aspect; everything was so wild yet so rich. We passed several clumps of poplar trees, but lying at their bases were scores of decayed and broken trunks. Presently a few houses sprang into view, we passed down a small avenue of poplars, through two high mud walls, and clattered into a square, in the middle, as a matter of fact, of the German colony.

Now if, instead of taking a drosky from Khiva to this place, twelve versts distant, I had gone up in a balloon and in the space of two hours had been dropped in some small German village in the heart of Bavaria, my feelings would perhaps have been about the same. I had already become accustomed to the Egyptian-like architecture of the Sart—here in this German colony were some thirty to forty small cottages German

U

in architecture to their very roofs. I saw for the first time chimneys. Here was a square, and there in the middle a huge well, and by the side a pair of large market scales.

The people crowded around my drosky to shake my hand and bid me welcome; people dressed in trousers and coats and German hats—white people speaking the language of the Fatherland. I went to Emile Reeson's cottage, a whitewashed edifice with a little sitting-room, a tiny bedroom, and a kitchen. Here Frau Reeson reigned supreme. Would I, asked the good housewife, have a cutlet, some white bread and butter, some asparagus— rather old, but, nevertheless, still good. I marvelled. Emile Reeson put on the airs of a host. He made me comfortable, he even brought down a bottle containing corn brandy, "schnapps," he called it, with a smile, and brought out one or two glasses, incidentally mentioning that such glasses were made in the colony, plates, knives, and forks, a snowy cloth to the table, tea in glasses, made by the agency of the Russian samover, from water (explained Emile Reeson) properly filtered. The Khirghiz dragoman looked upon all this with astonishment. It was the first time he had ever been invited to sit on a chair at a table. As a Khirghiz dragoman to his Excellency M. Galkin he was only a Khirghiz, and was happier on his haunches, with his legs crossed, and with a lump of meat in his fist at which he could gnaw, than sitting at a table. Emile Reeson possessed quite a little library of books. He well remembered, he said, the visit of Edward Moser, the Hungarian explorer, to Khiva some ten years previously, and it was apparent that Edward Moser had not forgotten the little German colony, for he had sent to Emile Reeson several volumes of the work he had published on his Central Asian experiences.

The meal finished, I made an exploration of the village, which was run on absolutely socialistic principles. Every man worked, and every man received the same amount of pay for so many hours' labour. The work consisted mainly of glass making and blowing, the fashioning of wooden and iron implements, and the making of wheels for arabas and carriages. Until the arrival of this little German colony at Khiva the Khan had not possessed a decent carriage, and one of his first orders to the Germans was for the construction of such a vehicle. So well did they acquit themselves in this task that several others of the principal Khivans ordered carriages, while a standing order from the Khan to the colony was the furbishing up once a year of the only gun which the city possessed. At the time of my visit this gun was undergoing its annual scouring and cleaning. It was a venerable piece, muzzle-loading and of brass, but the Khan revered it. It was the one he had had loaded when General von Kaufmann appeared before his gates, but which was never fired.

The Germans drove a brisk trade; in fact, they seemed to be the only artisans of any quality in or near Khiva. Their fame had spread, and from various towns of the province orders were received for different articles. I questioned Reeson as to what was the ambition of the colony, and the answer came pat. Everyone worked with an object, that object was at convenient intervals to send a family to America. Considering the great distance and the enormous expense, together with the scanty profit from their labour, this noble ambition bore but rare fruit. In the several years that had passed since the Germans followed Kaufmann into the wilds of Turkestan they had seen the futility of their hopes. Bad as must have been the condition of their fathers in their own land, it must have been ten thousand times better than this outcast life in Central Asia. A few poor families huddled together amidst a horde of barbarians in a climate which took them off one by one at an ever increasing rate. Their colonising endeavour had proved a failure. They had multiplied among themselves, it is true, but the original desire which dominated the colonists had not materialised, that is to say, the absolute subjugation of the Khanate and, with Russian intelligence and industry brought to bear, a big future for the early comers.

Emile Reeson took me down to the little graveyard of the colony, a graveyard all too well filled. He showed me, too, the little cottage where on Sundays he took his place as pastor, the cross on the wall in that country of absolute Mohammedanism speaking volumes.

They were contented with their lot, he said, such as it was. The laws which had been drawn up were such that it was impossible to be otherwise. They could not quarrel; no man was better than his fellow. They all obeyed the same regulations, and even he, as head-man, had to put in a certain amount of labour, intellectual or physical, so as to earn the bread he ate. His duty consisted principally of visiting Khiva and selling the manufactured goods to the Khan or the different potentates. There were others in the colony who showed special aptitude for wheel-making, shoe-making, and copper working, or glass making and blowing. Here, twelve versts from Khiva, was Edward Bellamy's socialistic dream in actual existence.

Khiva was reached at nightfall, and this I determined should be my last night there, in spite of the urgings of the Khirghiz dragoman to remain. He had, he said, to conduct several important missions concerning the administration of the province on the next day, but this I knew to be a lie, because M. Galkin had told me that the dragoman had nothing to do but look after me, and that I was to

THE GERMAN VILLAGE NEAR KHIVA

keep him by my side as much as possible, so that he would not have an opportunity of promiscuous chattering with the Khivans. I therefore gave orders for the drosky to be got ready on the following day, and, after passing a somewhat miserable night in the palace of Mat Murat, set out for Petro-Alexandrovsk at sunrise.

I can never remember leaving an important city with fewer regrets. I remember well the visits I have made to other Asiatic centres, where in some measure I have been charmed by this thing or that. Khiva held out no charms whatever. Instead, I had a feeling of gladness permeating me when a bend in the lane hid its walls from me. I saw even with gladness the disappearance of its round stunted tower on the horizon. Dust and morass had to be passed through before Khanki was reached. The heat of the day was spent on the platform of the hospitable Beg of Khanki, there was much feeding on figs and grapes and melons, slabs of pancake and pilau. In the afternoon the journey to the Amu-Daria, or Oxus, was resumed, and at about four o'clock the broad river came into view. I was anxious to reach Petro-Alexandrovsk. I had accomplished my mission, and it was my intention now to make haste to the south in order to join the trans-Caspian railroad near Bokhara, and so by way of Merv and Askabad reach the Caspian shore. *En route* to the Oxus I clinched my bargain with the driver of the drosky, who consented to take me over the intervening stretch of three hundred and fifty versts of desert to the first station on the trans-Caspian railroad for the sum of £22. As he was the only possessor of a tarantass and three horses in Petro-Alexandrovsk, it was that or nothing. I could wait, he said—and he was something of a humourist in his way—a couple of weeks for the steamboat, which took fifteen days to make the journey from Petro-Alexandrovsk to Charjui, that is if the steamboat did not get stuck in the sand. That meant a month's delay, while he—well, he guaranteed to get me to the railway inside five days from Petro-Alexandrovsk. I closed the bargain, glad almost at any price to be able to look forward to a speedy return to Europe.

I was not destined, however, to get back to

Petro-Alexandrovsk so quickly. When we arrived at the river bank we found a whole caravan of camels awaiting transportation across the river, and here I met an Afghan chieftain who spoke English, at least English understood after much trouble. He had been, said this Afghan, in Cabul, and jerked out words and sentences which told me he had been concerned in the war of '78; but he grasped my hand with great fervour and friendliness, mixed up his Afghan with his English in an unintelligible medley, meanwhile that my Khirghiz dragoman beamed upon us as if he had found for me a compatriot. All this occupied a long time, for it meant tea-drinking and talk. At length, however, we got aboard a flat-bottomed boat and the towers set off. For hours we struggled against the stream. Darkness came on and found us worming our way through the eddying waters, a dozen or more towers shouting, struggling, and splurging. Now and again we grounded on a sandbank, only to be got off by efforts which seemed superhuman. The darkness became deeper, stars blinked, and we grounded again.

"We'll have to stop here the night," said the

dragoman, "they have lost their way," and the towers came back to the boat, flinging themselves down in their exhaustion.   There was no help for it.   We were on the left bank, opposite Petro-Alexandrovsk it is true, but it was impossible in the darkness to hope to get across.   The banks were covered with tall reeds and grass, and, rather than sleep in the boat, I got the few rugs I had with me brought ashore.   To add to the dis-comfort of this enforced idleness we had not a scrap of food amongst us, and since leaving Khanki in the early afternoon my little escort had had nothing to eat.   It was while my things were being got out that I perceived away up the shore of the river a spark of light.   I directed the attention of the Khirghiz to it, and he sug-gested that we should go and find out what it was.   Off we went, pushing through the thickly-growing rushes and grass to come, after a few minutes' tramp, upon a small encampment by the side of the river, two Khivans snoring peace-fully by the side of a fire.   A kick from the Khirghiz roused one of the Khivans, and inquiries for food elicited replies in a negative sense.   The

Khivans had nothing to give us; they said they had nothing themselves, but I discovered a melon and seized it. One of the Khivans endeavoured to take it from me, but was buffeted back by the Khirghiz. Neither of us was in the mood for half measures. I wanted to give a few kopecks for the melon, but the Khirghiz told me it was unnecessary, and, as we were marching off, I fell headlong over a rope which stretched out into the water. Recovering myself I seized the rope, and what was my astonishment to find it was fast at the other end to something which was extremely lively. A fish, and that of some size without a doubt. I yelled to the Khirghiz to help me, but there came a rush on the part of the Khivans and we were knocked right and left.

To starve on the banks of the Oxus with a big fish on the end of a line was not to be thought of. We went back to our own encampment; we collected the twelve towers and the six men forming the escort, and in a solid body marched upon the camp of the enemy. It mattered little that the Khivans implored us to desist. We were in possession. They refused money as the purchasing equivalent for the huge sturgeon which was landed, or for the second sturgeon which was found on the end of another line. There was some rough play, and once I saw the gleam of a knife in the hands of one of the Khivans, but the odds were too uneven. The fish were killed and taken in triumph to our own camp. I forced a couple of silver roubles into the hand of one of the Khivans, which he promptly threw disdainfully on the ground. Back at the camp again we made a roaring fire, toasted bits of fish on the ends of long sticks, and ate them half raw and covered with wood smuts, without salt, but greedily.

It was noon on the following day before we reached Petro-Alexandrovsk. After Khiva that little town seemed a veritable paradise—the green and white church, the Russian magazines in the square, and the wooden buildings. The passage across the Oxus had taken us nearly four hours. My escort was paid off with liberal presents, the Khirghiz dragoman salaamed himself out of my presence, and I set to work to get my few belongings in order for the journey to the south.

THE KHAN

Thanks to the kindness of M. Galkin, an open letter was given me to the various head-men of the Turcoman and Bokharan tribes which I should have to pass through *en route* to Charjui. Ivan Sureseff promised that his tarantass and his three horses—horses which were beautiful to look upon, and the tarantass fit for the Czar—should be at my door on the following morning. I paid valedictory visits to the police-master, the doctor, and various other functionaries whose acquaintance I had made, and went to sleep that night to dream of Europe.

CHAPTER XXXI.

HOMEWARD

IVAN SURESEFF was as good as his word. His troika of horses and his tarantass duly appeared by six o'clock on the following morning, and away we went to the jangle of the douga bells. Petro-Alexandrovsk was soon left behind. We clattered through one or two small Khivan villages to pull up at the banks of the Oxus, where a boat took us across the stream and landed us on the edge of the trans-Caspian desert. Five days it was that Sureseff guaranteed to take me through to Charjui, but it was five days of strenuous labour for him, not to say some discomfort for myself, though that discomfort was minimised by the fact that instead of having a bicycle to ride through those hot and blistering sands I had now a tarantass to recline in, and was comforted by some show of good food and plenty of water.

From point to point we were accompanied by
two or three Khivans or Bokharans detailed off
by the various head-men of the towns. There
was no road or semblance of road. The sand
came to the very edge of the river, and we
found our way by following the banks. Sixty
or seventy miles above Khiva the Oxus runs
through a gorge-like channel, composed entirely
of sand and sandstone. Respectable hills appear
here and there, but not a vestige of vegetation
anywhere. Sterility is on every hand, except
where, in isolated spots, some village or town is
found luxuriating in a perfect oasis of vegetation.
We passed through the zone of Khivan influence
and entered that of the Turcomans. Turcomania
embraces practically the whole of trans-Caspia,
and although I had been promised adventures
from these nomadic and exceedingly truculent
people, none came to vary the monotony of the
sand and the heat. Some few Turcomans would
swoop down upon our little cavalcade now and
again, and at a respectful distance gaze curiously
at us. In the Bokharan towns I had the opportunity of seeing the difference between one set of

Mohammedans and the other. The Bokharans were more stalwart, more sprightly, more enterprising than their brethren of the north, turbaned and long-robed, blacker than the Khivans, and more lavish in their hospitality. Their towns were similar to those in the province of Khiva, but there was a greater display of orientalism, increasing day by day as we got further south.

The river narrowed and narrowed as the sand got worse. Our poor horses could only shuffle through the drifts, for after five days of incessant travel they were wearied beyond measure. There came the time, however, when Ivan Sureseff, whose company I had come to love in that journey, informed me that only another forty versts separated me from the road of iron, as he called it. This was on the morning of the sixth day. I became impatient for the sight of that civilising influence, the railway, and when at midday Sureseff begged for an hour for tea-drinking, I was hog enough to refuse him. On we went, the bells clanged and clattered, the horses stumbled and plunged through the sand. Trees appeared, long poplars and shady beeches. Out of the sand on to an earth road, huts and then houses sprang up to the right and the left. Magazines with Russian names were showing on each side. There came from a side street people dressed in Russian costume; not a Khivan shako to be seen, not a Bokharan turban, no flowing robes of the Oriental. Here was Russia—two gates across the road and a glimpse of shining metals between. A last jangle of the douga bells as Ivan pulled up his horses.

"Charjui, one of noble birth," said he. "God be praised, we have arrived."

I raided the nearest magazine. I bought a hat, a coat, and a bag, and made for the railway station without any ado.

"The first train," said the porter, "will arrive in twenty minutes' time."

"And the next?"

"In six days' time!"

Twenty minutes only for my stay in my first town bespeaking civilisation! But a stay of six days was not to be thought of. Poor Ivan Sureseff, he must have thought that I had gone crazy that I could have parted with him so

X

summarily, that I tore my belongings from the tarantass, threw out from this box and that various articles which I should now no longer require, paid him so hurriedly, and plunged on to the platform even as the train from Samarcand *en route* to the shores of the Caspian rolled in. Ten minutes' stoppage was the cry, ten minutes to give me a chance at a buffet on the station. I inquired curiously for a bottle of beer, and beer they gave me, the first opportunity of such since Orenburg. I got on the train, a strange train of white carriages and an oil-driven loco-motive, tipped the porter liberally to bring my baggage in. There were Jews and chinovniks and Russian merchants in my carriage *en route* to Europe. The train rolled out. I looked out of the window as we left the station and saw my last link with Khiva in the middle of the road— Ivan Sureseff, diligently counting the money I had given him. I only hoped I had not given him a rouble too little.

For two days that sluggish train thumped its way along the edge of the desert, and beneath what Persians and Afghans call the " edge of the world." There to the north stretched the undulating sea of sand, without one particle of green to relieve its yellow barrenness. There to the south, and seemingly within a stone's-throw, reared mighty mountains sheer out of the desert sands. The "edge of the world" they call it, and it looks like it. Beyond that cliff is the rolling country stretching straight away to the confines of India. What must be the thoughts of the southern dweller coming to the edge of those cliffs to see north of him nothing but those blinding sands?

Askabad—half an hour's pause, so that with incredible speed I promenaded wide and well-paved streets, saw at least twenty bicyclists careering on their way; omnibuses, cabs, and folks dressed in European costume. Here one was practically within shouting distance of Persia, yet here was a town as Russian as one could wish it. Back to the train, to notice with a smile the huddle of Bokharans on the platform, a few benighted Asiatics so out of place in their own home.

Merv, the great water depôt of the trans-

Caspian railroad, a bustling and thriving town, now having forgotten, perhaps, the time when it was the centre and the conflicting point of European politics—a water depôt supplying those huge tanks containing that necessary liquid for consumption by trans-Caspian railroad engines.

One morning soon after daybreak there was the shimmer of water. "Krasnovodsk!" exclaimed the chinovnik with whom I had chummed on this train journey, and, rounding a bend, the Caspian Sea spread itself before my gaze. Twenty-four hours later the paddle steamer from Krasnovodsk to Baku slid into dock in the great oil city. Here was industry and bustle if you like. Here Englishmen, Russians, Germans, and, in short, men of every nationality hustled each other in the race for wealth. Oil was spouting on these eastern slopes of the Caucasus, mineral wealth flowing at almost every drilling. A big smoky town, Baku, smelling evilly of paraffin; at night with the glare of burning fountains casting up reflections into the sky.

Then that ride over the Caucasus, through those misty blue mountains, where people in long

red cloaks, wearing cartridge cases on their breasts
and long daggers at their waists, came down to
gaze curiously at the train. Through canyons
dark and gloomy, through forests seemingly impenetrable, jerking and grinding slowly along,
round curves which it would seem to the accustomed eye impossible to negotiate.

Tiflis, a mass of white and brown houses,
hanging, apparently, on the .edge of a gigantic
cliff. Then the long, long plunge to the Black
Sea littoral; down and down with brakes creaking and wheels screeching. Level again till the
terminus was reached. Batoum! Arrived at
last, and able to stretch my legs in a walk
around the harbour, above which grim fortresses
rose, showing the gleam of cannon mouths here
and there, pointed arrogantly and almost menac-
ingly at the many little fluttering rags of flags
in the harbour, nine-tenths of them the Union
Jack.

I think I behaved myself rather foolishly on
my arrival at Batoum, for I went on board the
first English steamer, found an English sailor
meditatively smoking a pipe, and straightway

invited him to a drink. He came willingly enough, but he must have wondered, poor fellow, at the exuberance of one of his fellow-country-men; and maybe there goes on the deck of an English oil steamer in the Indian Ocean or by the coast of China a sailor who has met one English madman who has stood him as much drink as he could consume.

From Batoum to Constantinople, a five days' journey, during which we touched at Trebizond, Samsoun, and Ineboli, so that I was able to renew my acquaintance with Asia Minor, and to hear the old, old complaints of British residents concerning the iniquities of Abdul Hamed and his legions. Constantinople itself, with the usual grievances of its English population, the want of protection on the part of the British Government. Why on earth doesn't the Government capture the place, they ask plaintively, or do something so that ordinary British merchants can make their fortunes more rapidly? Strange, indeed, is the genus English trader abroad. He seems to imagine that he is there, not for his own good, but for the good of his country, and as an agent for the destruction of the country whose money he so skilfully absorbs.

En route to Marseilles, the Messageries Maritimes ship touched at Smyrna, where the Englishman thrives and fattens; at Athens, where Greeks look down their noses and appear disconsolate; at Crete, where a dozen warships in Suda Bay were then haggling about supremacy, and all that sort of thing. Through the Straits of Messina; the Straits of Bonifacio. The Chateau d'If came in sight one morning, a tempestuous morning, when big waves buffeted our vessel from side to side, and the entrance to Marseilles harbour was made difficult. There was the express train to Paris, and a swift journey by the banks of the Rhone. Lyon—Dijon—Paris! There was a drink or two at old resorts on well-known boulevards, and there was that rattletrap of a train to Calais; there was that miniature of a steamer to vibrate its way to Dover; there was a swift but genial Customs affair hard by the Admiralty Pier. And further, there was the maligned Chatham and Dover Railway, and the maligned Chatham and Dover train to hurtle its way through sunny and smiling Kent.

Familiar spires and familiar villages came and went. There were suggestions of metropolitan traffic in the neighbourhood of the Elephant and Castle Station. There was a sluggish river, barge laden and busy, making its oily way under the arches of Blackfriars Bridge. There was Holborn Viaduct at last, sloppy from a drizzling rain, and there were people who came forward to shake my hand and say, "Welcome back, old man!" and, under such circumstances as these, I became fully conscious that I had finished my adventure.

PLYMOUTH: WILLIAM BRENDON AND SON,
PRINTERS

www.ingramcontent.com/pod-product-compliance
Lightning Source LLC
LaVergne TN
LVHW012206040326
832903LV00003B/149